How To Be Led by the Holy Spirit

How To Be Led by the Holy Spirit

by
Norvel Hayes

Harrison House
Tulsa, Oklahoma

Unless otherwise indicated, all Scripture quotations are taken from the *King James Version* of the Bible.

2nd Printing
Over 25,000 in Print

How To Be Led by the Holy Spirit
ISBN 0-89274-731-5
Copyright © 1996 by Norvel Hayes
P. O. Box 1379
Cleveland, Tennessee 37311

Published by Harrison House, Inc.
P. O. Box 35035
Tulsa, Oklahoma 74153

Contents

1
Renew Your Mind

So then with the mind I myself serve the law of God; but with the flesh the law of sin.

Romans 7:25

The average Christian is led by the Spirit of God probably only about half of their life simply because they don't know how to follow Him. In other words, most people are not led by the Spirit of God. You would probably know that if you were around them very much. Of course, people who live in sin and don't know the Lord Jesus Christ can't be led by the Spirit of God because He doesn't live inside of them.

Be Reborn

In order to be led by the Spirit, you must first of all know that God is a Spirit. (John 4:24.) Therefore, He must lead you by His Spirit. And since you are made in the image of God (Gen. 1:27), you are a spirit as well. You *have* a soul, and you *live* in a body, but you *are* a spirit.

But until your spirit has been reborn by God, the things of God will be foolishness to you. (1 Cor. 1:27.) You will never be able to hear God and be led by the Spirit of God because you won't be able to see the value in the things that God has to say or the things that God wants you to do. Until your spirit has been reborn by God, you will not be able to enjoy the benefits that God has for you.

Once your spirit is reborn, you have a right to the things that are in the Bible. God wrote the Bible for you. But do you know that the average Christian has never really understood that everything from Matthew through Revelation is for them? Financial success is for them. Spiritual success is for them. A well body is for them. A clear mind is for them. Peace that the natural man can't understand is for them. It is in the Bible, and it is for them. Everything that heaven has to offer is for them.

Unfortunately most Christians, even though they belong to God and basically love God and would go to heaven if they died, are all mixed up. They don't know what belongs to them and what doesn't belong to them; neither do they know how to get it. They think, "Well, I'll just go to church, and if it happens to me, okay. I'll just let it happen. And if it doesn't happen, then it wasn't supposed to happen to me." Now that is about as far from the truth as you can possibly ever get!

You will never be able to get your thinking straightened out until you get your spirit straightened out. I can't do it for you, but I can teach you what the Lord has taught me.

Listen to the Spirit

First of all, I want to explain to you why Jesus responds to human beings. The Holy Spirit of God leads Jesus to respond to you. When you go to Jesus and give Him chapter and verse, then He goes to the Father and presents your case to Him using chapter and verse.

See, when you are reborn, the Greater One lives inside you. He speaks to your spirit. Jesus really doesn't speak to you directly. We may say that He does sometimes, but He really doesn't. He speaks to the Holy Spirit on the inside of you, then the Holy Spirit speaks to your reborn human spirit, and you speak out what He has told you and bring it into existence through the words that you speak.

But if you don't listen to Him, then He can't get it over to you, and you miss God. Do you understand that? Jesus

Himself was led by the Spirit of God when He walked on this earth as a man. He lived in a body that had bones and blood just like yours and mine do. But unlike you and me, He chose to be led by the Spirit of God in every decision. Romans 8:11 says that the same Spirit that was in Him is in you. But to walk like Jesus walked, you have to be willing to be led by the Spirit of God in every decision.

Unfortunately some people are in the habit of doing what they want to do and speaking out what they want to speak. They say to themselves, "This is what I'll do." They might as well go ahead and do it because they aren't going to be led by their spirit anyway! They have already made up their mind what they are going to do.

We are our own worst enemy. Everybody is their own worst enemy. Jesus is not your enemy. The Spirit of God Who lives inside of you is not your enemy. He wants to lead you. He wants to impart things to your spirit that will bring you great and mighty blessings — not just spiritually, but financially, mentally and emotionally as well. He wants to bring you great blessings, but you must listen to Him. That is why He wants you to do what He tells you.

Serve the Law of God

Now there are some things that you don't have to be led by the Spirit in because the Bible plainly states that you should just go ahead and do them. Take praying for instance. You don't have to be led by the Spirit of God to pray. God has already told you in the Bible to do that, so all you have to do is go ahead and do it. When it comes to bringing sinners to church with you, you don't have to be led by the Spirit of God because He has already told you to do that.

Unfortunately many Christians don't pray very much nor do they bring sinners to church. That is because they would rather follow their flesh than follow their spirit. In

Romans 7:24, the Bible says, **O wretched man that I am! who shall deliver me from the body of this death?** I can tell you Who will deliver you because there is only one Deliverer, and that is Jesus Christ our Lord. There aren't three or four Deliverers. There is only one. And that is exactly what verse 25 says, **I thank God through Jesus Christ our Lord.**

Verse 25 continues: **So then with the mind I myself serve the law of God; but with the flesh the law of sin.** That is right. You are either a servant to the law of God, or you are a servant to the law of the flesh.

Now how would this apply to your life? If you were sick and you let your mind wander around and give your body all the attention, then you would become a servant to the law of the flesh, and eventually it would cost you your life. You would die because that is sin in the eyes of God. Do you understand that? It would be sin for you to give all of your attention to what your body is doing and how your flesh is reacting and what happens to your flesh. That isn't what God wants you to be thinking about.

God wants your mind renewed with the Word of God *all the time* so you can believe Him. Unless you keep your mind renewed with God's Word, then you can't even believe the book of Matthew. All you will do is read it because it is a nice book and because you have been told to read it for the last thirty years. You may think it is the right thing to do because your grandma told you, so you just kind of read it every now and then, but you don't really have any earthly idea what is in there.

You can ask most people who have read the Bible for thirty years some questions about the Bible, and they will respond by saying, "Oh, is that in there?" Then when the devil comes to destroy them, they are in a fix because all they did was read the Bible without confessing it and making it a part of themselves.

Always remember this, "The devil is coming, and he is coming to tempt you, to get you to yield to some fleshly lust or disease. But if you will keep your mind renewed with the Word of God, you will serve God according to His law, and you will turn your mind over to the law of God. Now if you don't keep your mind renewed with the Word of God, you will serve anything that comes along that disturbs you, especially your body.

If you give so much attention to your flesh that you aren't able to keep your mind in good enough shape so that it can receive the law of God, then you are serving the law of flesh, and it is sin in the eyes of God. If you don't keep your mind renewed with the law of God, which is the Word of God, then you can't even obey the law of God. If you are going to think in the flesh realm and worry about your body all of the time, then you are already in death and don't even know it.

On the other hand, if you will serve the Lord Jesus Christ with your mind, according to His Word, you will obey the law of God.

Your Mind Is Important, Too!

But you will have to serve God with your mind as well as your spirit. Did you know that? Unfortunately a lot of full-gospel people will get baptized with the Holy Ghost and get on fire for God and win souls for Jesus, but after five, ten, fifteen years, it gets to be an old thing to them, and they stop praying in tongues so much anymore. They don't worship Jesus very much any more. The Holy Ghost is still inside them because He won't ever leave them, but their minds get squirrely, and they start making goofy decisions. The only reason they start making goofy decisions is because they aren't praying in tongues as much as they should in their prayer life, and they aren't reading their Bible enough to keep their mind renewed with the Word of God.

11

So what happens? They turn their mind loose in a world of darkness where all the devil gives them are thoughts and suggestions that have something to do with their body or what they want. He will especially come to try and fill some empty spot or vacuum in your life. And because you aren't listening to your spirit, you will begin to make squirrely decisions.

Pretty soon you will be saying, "Oh, the piano player looks so beautiful. The woman next door looks so beautiful." She could be a scuzzball, and you don't know it. I talk to men sometimes who come in for counseling. Some of them look like they have just been rung out like a rag and come in saying, "I divorced my wife ten years ago, and I married this woman, and I have lived in a hell ever since. I don't know why I did it. She wasn't what I thought she was after I married her." Now do you understand why I'm still single?

Unless you serve the law of God with your mind, you won't even listen to the Holy Spirit on the inside of you. But if you will keep your mind renewed with the Word of God, you can be led by the Spirit.

Get the Scriptures in Your Spirit

Not only must your mind be renewed with the Scriptures, but you must also get them into your spirit. The Bible says that the kingdom of God is within you. (Luke 17:21.) In other words, you are only one statement away from all the blessings that are in heaven for you. You are only one verse of Scripture away from success in the area that you have not been successful in. You are just one verse of Scripture away, not five or six. You are just one!

Now if you were to sit down and take a piece of paper and list one, two, three, four, five, six, seven, eight, nine, ten of the different areas of your life that you are not successful in, then go through the New Testament from Matthew to

Revelation looking up Scriptures to cover each one of them, you will find out the blessings God has for you.

Mark that Scripture in your Bible, write it out or type it out on a piece of paper and memorize it so that you can get it into your spirit. To make a Scripture a part of you, you have to quote it from your mouth hundreds and hundreds of times. You have to memorize it. Until you do, it will not become a part of you. It will only be something you have heard, and we all have heard a particular Scripture at one time or another. But unless you make that particular Scripture a part of you, you cannot be led by the Spirit of God in that particular area.

Any sick person in the world is just one healing Scripture away from remaining sick or dying. Some people may say, "Brother Norvel, you came to our church and you prayed for sick people every day, but on Monday morning I've lost the manifestation of the healing."

You must hold fast to the things that you receive from God! How can you hold fast to them? You hold fast by the blood of the Lamb and the word of your testimony. (Rev. 12:11.) You have to hold fast like a tiger that is hungry and gets a hold of a piece of meat. He holds fast to it because he is hungry. He says, "You aren't going to get this. You aren't going to get this." The devil is going to come and try to steal anything you get from God away from you. (John 10:10.) He even tried to tempt and steal from Jesus!

Right after Jesus' baptism, the Spirit led Him into the wilderness where the devil tempted Jesus. It was after Jesus had prayed and fasted in the mountains for forty days and forty nights that the devil appeared to Him in person and said, "If You're really the Son of God, why don't You change these stones into bread?" And Jesus said, "It is written." Then the devil said, "Well, uh, let me show You something else I want to give You." Jesus said, "It is written." Then the devil said, "Yes, but I'll take You up on the high pinnacle, and I'll show You all the things of the world, and I'll give You everything that you see if You will bow down and worship me." Jesus said, "It is written and besides that — get away from Me!" (Matt. 4:1-11, author's paraphrase.)

Then the Bible says that the devil left Jesus, and the angels from heaven came and began to minister to Him. (Matt. 4:11.) Jesus told the devil three times in his face, "It is written." Finally the devil got the message and left. You can see from this Bible account the reason why God wants you to become a Bible reader and a Bible believer who quotes the Word out of your mouth. But until you get those words in your spirit, you will never quote them out of your mouth. Jesus wants you to speak the Word so that the devil won't steal from you.

Find a True New Testament Church

You and I are supposed to serve God according to the Bible, not according to some religious concept that you may have or the church you go to may have about God. Very few churches are true New Testament churches. You won't find very many churches who will carry food to the poor and take up money to help the widows and divorcees who have little children. You won't find many churches that will help the elderly either. You won't find your town overloaded with churches that have those kinds of programs set up. Most of them don't even have a witnessing program to win souls for God!

You may say, "What *do* they have?" I don't know. I guess they just do their own thing. "Then what happens to them?" Eventually they slip out of the deep blessing of the Lord, and that isn't the way God ever intended it to be. God's Church should be flowing in the blessing of God all of the time. Now any church can do their part. They can at least make a standing effort to help people in their time of need. The Bible tells us to do that.

But if the people in the church don't keep their minds renewed with the Word of God, they will not obey the law of God with their mind, and as a result their decisions will not be high quality. They will be tempted to obey only themselves and to do what their friends think they should do, and they will let their minds wonder. God wants them to obey His law with their minds. He wants them to keep their minds renewed with the Word of God and to bring heaven down to earth with their thinking.

Don't Be Deceived

Unfortunately there are all kinds of spirits trying to lead people, and they do lead them. In the latter times, there is a spirit that will work to deceive, but you must learn to be led by the Spirit of God. First Timothy 4:1 talks about seducing spirits and doctrines of devils that will be at work to cause some to depart from the faith. Unfortunately many people are led by spirits that they think are the Holy Spirit, but they aren't, and they will only find it out when they die and stand before God.

The Holy Spirit always leads people in line with the Bible. Always remember, Jesus never changes. If you ever go into a church service where they try to change the Jesus that you know is in the New Testament, you are in the wrong kind of church because Jesus never changes. God never changes. The Bible says that God cannot lie, and the Bible says that God does not change.

If you can show me in the New Testament where Jesus ever healed one sick person, He will heal you. And if He doesn't, then He has changed. But the Bible says He has not changed and isn't going to change. (Heb. 13:8.) And until you believe He hasn't changed, you won't see a cripple get up out of a wheelchair and walk off. When you know God well enough, you will be able to look at a man in a wheelchair and say, "Jesus wants to stretch your legs out."

You have to tell him that. If you don't tell him, he won't believe it, and he will sit there and die a cripple.

Some people say they don't believe in miracles because they have never seen one. People like this say, "I never saw Jesus perform any miracles. I never saw Jesus open the eyes of a blind man. I never saw Jesus heal a crippled man. I never saw Jesus do any of that!" Or they say, "I believe Jesus performed miracles then, but I don't believe He will do it now." As long as they talk like that, they never will see anything.

Do you know why? Because the Holy Spirit doesn't agree with their mouth. The Holy Spirit agrees only with the Bible. The Spirit and the Word agree. Now if you want the Holy Spirit to do something for you, you have to make up your mind to believe the Bible.

When you try to change the Jesus Who is in the Bible, then you are in trouble. You may float along in this life, but you will never see the supernatural power of God. Jesus actually does want to stretch out legs and heal diseases. And if you will begin to believe it, He will do it, but God demands your believing. He requires your faith.

Even the men who walked with Jesus and saw the miracles didn't really know Him. They tried to get blind Bartimaeus to be quiet, but he didn't pay any attention to them. He just kept on crying, "Jesus, Son of David, have mercy on me! Jesus, Son of David, have mercy on me!"

Jesus stopped and said, "Those cries are cries of faith! Bring that man who is crying to Me. I command you," Jesus said, "to bring him to Me!" (Author's paraphrase.) He didn't say, "If you want to, bring him to Me." No, He said, "I command you to bring him to Me." And they brought blind Bartimaeus to Jesus.

And Jesus said, "What do you want Me to do for you?" And he said, "That I may see, Jesus. That I may see. Open up my eyes that I may see, Jesus." Jesus said, "Your faith has healed you." (Mark 10:46-52, author's paraphrase.)

Now I am not writing about what the people who walked with Jesus did, and I am not talking about what you believe or what somebody else believes. I am writing about what the Bible says about Jesus. There is only one Jesus, and He is the One Who is in the New Testament from Matthew through Revelation. And the Bible says that the Jesus I know healed blind Bartimaeus.

The Lord will heal *you* if you will show Him some faith and do what He said to do. But as long as you fight the Bible and refuse to believe, you won't get the Holy Spirit to agree with you. And if you don't believe that, then the Holy Spirit can never help you because the Holy Spirit works only in line with the Bible.

If you make up your mind that you will believe the Bible and that Jesus is the same yesterday, today and forever, then He will begin to lead you by His Holy Spirit into all the blessings that heaven has for you. God never changes. (Mal. 3:6.)

2

Worship the Lord

And when he saw [Jesus], he fell at his feet.
Mark 5:22

If you really want to be led by the Holy Spirit, you must not only renew your mind with the Word of God, but you must also spend time worshipping Him. When was the last time you fell on your face and worshipped the Lord? You might say, "Am I supposed to do that?" If you have Scripture for it you are. "What is that for?" It is a sign of respect and reverence that says He is God, and you are nothing in comparison to Him. God said in Isaiah 55:9: **For as the heavens are higher than the earth, so are my ways higher than your ways, and my thoughts than your thoughts.**

You don't know everything, and I don't know everything, but I have good news for you — the Holy Spirit does. He knows everything, and He lives inside of you and me. He knows everything, and He knows how to do everything. I don't know how to do everything, but I have the One inside of me Who knows how to. Now I don't hear Him one hundred percent of the time, but I sure do listen to Him a lot more than I used to, and I hit more now than I miss.

Listen to what He is saying to you. Approach God reverently by spending time worshipping Him. Spend time in prayer so that you can get your spirit in shape. God is a God Who wants to be worshipped, and you need to worship Him. God wants you to worship Him, but you don't need to worship Him just for His sake. No, you need to worship God for your own sake because you are made to worship Him.

He is a God Who loves the praises of His people, and He wants to be worshipped. He wants to be praised. He wants to see you doing it. And you are a human being who is desperate to worship God. Jairus was a man who was desperate to worship God, and he was willing to fall on his face and worship God even though a crowd of people were standing around. He wasn't ashamed. His daughter was dying, and he needed help. Mark 5:22 says that the first thing he did was to worship Jesus: **And, behold, there cometh one of the rulers of the synagogue, Jairus by name; and when he saw** him [Jesus], **he fell at his feet.**

Build Your Spirit Up

If I can teach you to value the important things, things will be real easy for you. I don't have any sad days or wondering days, and you won't have very many of them either if you will spend more time worshipping God and praying in the spirit, praying in tongues. By worshipping God and praying, you keep your spirit built up, and that is your responsibility. No one can make you do that. God can't make you do that. That is something that you will have to choose to do yourself. You will have to pray in the Spirit yourself. You will have to keep your spirit built up.

Building your spirit and your faith up is like building a house, but you have to know what to do. Paul said in First Corinthians 14:18, **I thank my God, I speak with tongues more than ye all.** In First Corinthians 14:4, he says that speaking in tongues edifies you or builds you up. Jude 20 says you build yourself up on your most holy faith, praying in the Holy Ghost. Now if you don't keep your spirit built up in God, how in the world are you going to listen to Him?

Remember, God is a Spirit (John 4:24), and He is inside of you.

Do you remember when you got saved? The Spirit of God was coming up out of you, and you were laughing and crying all at the same time, and the love of God was all over you? Do you remember how sweet you felt? You didn't ever want to say a harmful word to anybody the rest of your life, and you couldn't stop telling Jesus how much you loved Him. That is the way He wants you to be all the time.

You may say, "That's right, Brother Norvel, but as soon as He leaves, I turn back into an animal." But that is you. That is not the Lord. That is you, and you aren't being led by the Spirit of God. You may say, "What am I supposed to do if I say things I shouldn't?" Cut off the talking. Smack yourself in the mouth, and don't talk. You may say, "But, Brother Norvel, I can't help myself. I've been doing this so long I can't help myself. It's like a habit to me."

The first three or four times you blow your stack, go somewhere and fall on your knees before God just like Jairus did and ask the Holy Spirit to remove that thing out of you. I got rid of junk like that by taking authority over it. I would say, "You foul spirit of temper, in Jesus' name, come out of me. You foul spirit of temper, I take authority over you. In Jesus' name, get out of me; get out of me; get out of me. You foul spirit of temper go from me; go from me; go from me. You foul spirit of temper, you have no authority over me; go from me; get out of me!" Foul spirits get afraid of you when you don't have any quitting sense, and they run from you.

Submit Yourself to God

The Bible says in James 4:7, **Submit yourselves therefore to God. Resist the devil, and he will flee from you.** You have to resist the devil. You are living in a world that God doesn't control. He only controls the Holy Spirit and the Bible and you, if you will listen to the Bible.

See, the devil is the god of this world, and he doesn't give up on you easily. If you think you are just going to float around after you get saved, just float through the devil's world and have all the good things from heaven drop on you, then you are in for a real surprise.

I am going to tell you right up front, if you ever start doing anything for God, if you ever even start passing out tracts for God, the devil will turn hordes and herds of demons loose on you. And if you don't watch it, the demons that operated through you before will come back in you again. He will sic them on you just like siccing dogs after rabbits. That is the way the devil will do you if you ever start doing anything for God. He will try to discourage you so that you won't persist and hang around for the blessings.

Resist the Devil

Did you know that the devil tries to talk people out of doing anything for God? If you don't believe me, go out sometime and try it. Get some tracts, then go out and knock on a few doors. The first bad reception you get, the devil will blast you. I mean he will blast you. Where at? He will blast your natural mind. But you have to learn to not listen to your natural mind. It doesn't make any difference what he tells you. Every time you go anywhere and start doing anything for God, the devil will blast your natural mind and say, "This is not your bag. This is not for you." The first time somebody opens up the door and says gruffly, "Yes, what do you want!" You will timidly respond, "Well, I want to talk to you about the Lord."

"The Lord! I don't even believe in him!"

"Oh, well, okay."

On the way back to your car, the devil will say to you, "This is not your ministry, you dummy. Go home and watch Christian TV, but don't go knocking on any doors. This is not your ministry. You are supposed to be watching TV."

The devil doesn't mind you watching a preacher on TV because he gives a message of salvation when you are already saved. The devil is sneaky, and you have to watch him. He wants to keep you in the natural, but you have to bombard him by stepping out of the natural and listening to what the Spirit of God is saying to you. When you obey God and do things for Him, His blessings will totally fall on you.

Show God Reverence

Mark 5:22 tells us that Jairus fell down at Jesus' feet. Jairus was a desperate human being. Does God help desperate human beings? He helps them when they come to Him like they are supposed to and recognize that He is God. You can't have a desperate situation in your home or your family and say, "If God wants to do this for me, then He will." No! He won't do it unless you make up your mind to come to Him reverently first of all and know that He is God because the Bible says, **He that cometh to God must believe that he is, and that he is a rewarder of them that diligently seek him** (Heb. 11:6).

If you want victory, you can't come to God with a nonchalant attitude and keep doing your own thing, saying, "Well, God, I'll go to church just to see what might happen. I'm not sure You are real, but I'll go just in case. I don't believe anything is going to happen, but I'll go to satisfy You."

If you want victory, you will have to show God reverence. If you want Jesus to respond, show reverence toward God and say,"I worship You, Jesus. I come before

You, God, and I worship You. I praise You, God. Lord, I'm not coming to You today for anything. I'm just going to take some time out of my life to come to worship You because I love You and because You are my Father and I am your child. I worship You, oh, God. I praise You, oh, God. I just come to worship You and to stay awhile in Your holy presence. I just want to worship You, God, because You are a great God. Oh, Jesus, I love You, and I praise Your wonderful blessed name."

One time the Lord showed me that many Christians miss His blessings because they hardly spend any time worshipping Him. You don't have to believe what I tell you, but believe it when you read it in the Bible, and you spend some time worshipping the God Who made you. That should be why you go to church — to worship and to praise Him, not to listen to man's doctrine or to man's ideas. God owns the church. Men aren't supposed to run the church. God is supposed to run the church. Jesus is the Head of the Church, not men. You need to go to church and worship the God Who loves you. People who don't go to church and people who rarely pray — people who don't worship God — aren't going to be very blessed by God.

Worship When No One Is Looking

If I could talk you into worshipping Jesus not only in church but also in your room where nobody sees you, then the Lord would give you anything you ask for in His will (1 John 5:14,15) like He does for me. You could have anything you wanted. One time the Lord spoke to me and said, "Son, if you'll talk people into worshipping Me when nobody is looking at them, I will reward them openly. The greatest thing that I ever see is when I look down and see one of my children worshipping Me when they are by themselves."

It's easy to worship along with a great worship team in a service. A great worship team could get even a sinner to worship God because they have a ministry along that line! Sure, God raises up people to minister in worship for the body of Christ, but what God really wants you to do is to take what you learned in that service home with you. He wants you to take it to your bedroom or to your office and worship Him without shame on your own.

Tell God You Love Him

Do you realize that the greatest commandment is to love the Lord? Do you know how it makes God feel when you tell Him that you love Him? You might say, "Brother Norvel, I live a clean life, and the Lord knows I love Him." That's good, but it isn't good enough. The commandment that sums up all the others says, **Thou shalt love the Lord thy God with all thy heart, and with all thy soul, and with all thy strength, and with all thy mind** (Luke 10:27). In other words, you need to fulfill the first commandment, **Thou shalt have no other gods before me** [God] (Ex. 20:3).

If you can tell your girlfriend or boyfriend, your husband or your wife and your children, why can't you tell God that you love Him? I love to walk back and forth across the floor sometimes, not asking God for anything, but just telling Him that I love Him.

Make a decision right now to obey the first commandment. Just close your eyes and hold your hands up to the Lord like a little child and say, "I love You, Jesus. I love You, Jesus. I love You, Jesus." You making that one statement is better than gold. When you make that statement over and over and over again, it will eventually become a part of you. So say, "I love You, Jesus. I love You, Jesus. Help me, Lord, to do Your work. I love You, Jesus. I love You, Jesus. I love the Gospel, Jesus. It is the power of God unto salvation, to everyone that believeth. I love the Gospel, Jesus. I love You, Jesus. I love You, Jesus. I love You, Jesus.

Now, change it a little bit and say, "Jesus, I love the Bible. Jesus, I love the Bible. Jesus, I love the Bible. Thank You, Lord, for giving me Your Word. Thank You, Lord, for giving me life. Thank You, Lord. Glory be to God."

If the Spirit of God begins to come upon you while you are worshipping Him and you feel like weeping before Him, then go ahead and weep. Just yield yourself to Him. He knows You love Him, but He likes you to tell Him so. Tell Him so today, and just let Him bless you.

3
Walk by Faith

Be not afraid, only believe.

Mark 5:36

Now there are two things that Jairus has done so far that
have pleased Jesus. The first thing he did was to fall down
at Jesus' feet and show reverence to Him. The second thing
he did was to ask Jesus to do something by faith. We know
it is by faith because of what he said in Mark 5:23, **My little
daughter lieth at the point of death: I pray thee, come and
lay thy hands on her, that she may be healed; and she
shall live.**

Ask by Faith

Did you ever do that? Some people may answer, "Uh,
no, I never did do that, Brother Norvel. That isn't what
makes it work for you, is it?" Listen, if you have a sick child
and the minister comes to pray for your child, then say,
"Come on in my house. You are welcome here in the name
of the Lord. Come in here and lay your hands on my child,
and we will agree that my child will be healed."

Those are the kind of words that are supposed to come
out of *your mouth*. You are supposed to make that statement
yourself. Most people end up saying something like,
"Come over and pray for my daughter, and I hope the Lord
will heal her when you come." Hebrews 11:6 says, **But
without faith it is impossible to please him [God]: for he
that cometh to God must believe that he is, and that he is a
rewarder of them that diligently seek him.** You need to be
talking in faith to please God! Instead of saying, "Well, I

hope the Lord will heal her....," why don't you just be quiet until you get the Bible in your spirit? If you would just be quiet, you would be better off because other people's faith could work for you a little bit.

God doesn't want you to be quiet. When you sit down and learn what the Bible says, quote Scripture and talk like this man Jairus talked, God will answer you. How did Jairus talk? He spoke words of faith, and they were scriptural. They referred to a doctrine of the church. He didn't say, "Maybe she will live, or I hope she will live." He said, "And she shall live." These are four of the most important words that he said.

Base Your Request on God's Word

Remember this: you can't approach God with religious ideas and religious statements. You need chapter and verse. Jairus spoke in faith on a doctrine of the Church. What is a doctrine of the Church? There are several. Salvation and baptism by water are doctrines of the Church. The laying on of hands is a doctrine of the Church.

If you don't believe me, look at the examples in the New Testament. Healing is all through the New Testament. Those were doctrines of the New Testament Church. With a doctrine, you don't have a choice whether to do it if you want to. You do it because it is a doctrine of the Church. In other words, I am telling you boldly right now that any church in America that does not have the ministry of laying on of hands is out of God's will. Is that clear? They are not obeying the Bible. I don't care what type of church they are, they don't have the right to decide which doctrines they want to apply and which ones they don't want to apply.

Most all churches baptize with water in one fashion or another. Most all churches have that doctrine, and that is correct. Why, then, can't all churches apply the doctrine of laying on of hands?

Let me explain something to you. I was raised in a church that had the doctrine of baptism with water and the doctrine of the laying on of hands. As a matter of fact, of the thirteen or fourteen million members around the world, every member probably knows about the doctrine of the laying on of hands.

You might ask, "Do they ever apply it in that type of church?" Sure, they apply it, but only on one occasion — the time of ordination. When a young man is called to preach in that type of church, several ministers must come into agreement that he is called and that he should be ordained. They question him, then have an ordination service where they ordain him to preach so he can get his papers.

At the ordination service, they gather around him, lay hands on him and pray for him, then send him out to preach the Gospel of the Lord Jesus Christ. And that is scriptural. But they don't use the ministry of the laying on of hands for sick people, yet it is a doctrine of the Church that Jesus used. It is a scriptural doctrine, a good, solid, Bible doctrine. That church does it when someone is ordained, but not for sick people, which is not correct. They need to lay hands on sick people.

In truth, they are disobeying the Lord Jesus Christ because Jesus said in Mark 16:18, **They shall lay hands on the sick, and they shall recover.** God even used Paul's hands to perform miracles. Acts 19:11,12 says:

> **And God wrought special miracles by the hands of Paul:**
>
> **So that from his body were brought unto the sick handkerchiefs or aprons, and the diseases departed from them, and the evil spirits went out of them.**

Lay hands on cloths and aprons and handkerchiefs and put them on sick bodies? You may say, "Maybe that is what they did then, but does it work today?" Why, sure it works today! It is in the New Testament, isn't it? Everything in the New Testament works today. Did you know that? We are supposed to have all the doctrines of the New Testament operating in the Church, not just part of them. God didn't write the New Testament so we could have part of it. He wrote the New Testament so we could have all of it — every doctrine and every chapter and verse!

Go by Faith, Not by Feelings

Now someone may say, "Brother Norvel, I've had hands laid on me, but I didn't feel anything." Jesus said, "Lay your hands on the sick, and they shall recover" (Mark 16:18, author's paraphrase.) What do feelings have to do with it? All you have to do is believe.

Not long ago in the Indianapolis, Indiana convention center, a girl was sitting in a wheelchair over against the wall. After hands were laid on her, she continued to sit there for about five to ten minutes. Then all of a sudden while she was sitting there, the Spirit of God began to deal with her, and she got up and walked.

I have seen people come down to the front of the church to have hands laid on them and watched them hobble back up the walkway to their seat. Then when the Spirit of God falls upon them, I've seen them throw their crutches down and just start walking.

One time when I was speaking at the same service, two people left their wheelchairs even before we started the service. People were so ready to be healed that Jesus started healing them in the hallway while they were on their way to church. That is the way I like to see it.

God doesn't deal with you according to what I believe. He deals with you according to your faith. You receive according to your faith. You may say, "I don't believe those

Scriptures." Then the laying on of hands isn't going to help you. I could lay my hands on you until all your hair fell out, but it still wouldn't help you because you didn't believe to start with.

The healing power of Jesus works in strange ways. I remember one time when I was teaching the Bible and the Lord said to me, "I want you to teach tonight on healing by faith with no feelings." So I taught that night on healing by faith and just simply believing what the Bible says.

People came up, I laid my hands on them, and it looked like nobody received anything from God. One man who had been a runner had to wear a brace on his leg just to walk. He hadn't run in years.

After I finished praying for him, I walked in front of all of them and said to them, "Why are you healed?" They said, "Because I obeyed the Bible." Then I said again, "Why are you healed?" And they said, "Because I obeyed the Bible."

When the church service was over, the man who had been a runner went home and went to bed. He never felt a thing, but the next morning he woke up, pushed the cover back, slung his legs over on the side of his bed and put his feet on the floor. When he looked down at his leg, it was completely whole! He put on his shoes, walked outside and ran a mile.

When he told all of this, I asked him if he had felt anything from the time I laid my hands on him until this moment, and he said, "No, not one thing." He simply *believed* the Scriptures, and Jesus made his leg whole while he was sleeping. He acted by faith.

Jesus' Response

Now notice how Jesus responds to Jairus' faith in Mark 5:24: **And Jesus went with him.** Jesus will always go with you when you apply the Scriptures. You might say, "What do you mean, 'go with you'? He is already in me!" I know He is. He will never leave you nor forsake you (Heb. 13:5), but I am not talking about that. When I say that He will be with you, I mean that He will begin to manifest Himself through you because He will be taking those words you speak in line with the Scriptures to God.

Jesus, in the last chapter of Mark, said, "I'm going to heaven to sit on the right hand of the Father and work with you according to the Scriptures, confirming the Word with signs following." (Mark 16:19,20, author's paraphrase.)

Do you know that God the Father releases His power to you only if Jesus brings Him the correct information from your mouth? And your prayer, my brother or sister, might not be the correct information. It all depends on if you are applying the Scriptures. What the Scriptures say are promised to you.

If you didn't receive that thing that you were looking for from God, then spend that time hunting for chapter and verse rather than hollering, "Oh, God, why me?" Spend your time standing steadfast on God's Word and not wavering. Don't expect someone else to do it for you. You do it yourself!

My brother or sister, when you were born again by the Spirit of God, you became a member of God's Church, the Body of Christ. You aren't some little, old puppet that lives down here on Spruce Street. That isn't who you are! You are a king and priest in Christ Jesus (Rev. 5:10), and you have a right to stand up straight, walk straight, smile straight, talk straight and claim what you need from God, but you must come to Him reverently and show Him respect by quoting the Bible and expecting to receive.

Then Jesus will walk before the Father, with chapter and verse, and say, "Your child has a need and this is the

Scripture he" (or "she") "is standing on." Then God will say, "Let it be said, and let it be done." And when God says, "Let it be done," my brother or sister, defeat is all over. God's power will come and flow through your body and drive out disease. God's power will come into your crooked leg and stretch your leg out. God's power will give you a new heart.

But you must come to the place that you can keep your words in order. Otherwise, you aren't going to receive anything from God. All you are going to do is live in a world of wondering. You will be wondering, "How did I get here? Why don't good things happen to me? Why am I broke?" And the next time I see you, do you know what you will be? You will be a wonderer, just like you are right now.

You have to learn as quickly as you possibly can to be sure and watch your mouth because that thing will not only get you in trouble; it will keep you in trouble. The Bible won't even work for you. Even though you may basically love God, the Bible won't work for you if you don't watch your mouth.

Jesus said in Matthew 12:34, **For out of the abundance of the heart the mouth speaketh.** The Lord told me one time, "Son, you don't have to judge people." I thought He was going to correct me when He said that. I thought I had been judging them too strong, but instead, He taught me something. He said, "You don't have to judge anybody. Just listen to them and their mouth will always judge them."

Did you know that? Your mouth will always tell the condition of your spirit. What comes out of your mouth is what is in your spirit. You can't speak it out unless it is in there. It reveals who you are and what condition you are in. If you want to find out how much this pastor down the street or that pastor on the other side of town knows about God, just go listen to him, and you will know by the words coming out of his mouth.

Accept Nothing But Victory

Now go back to Mark 5:24:

And Jesus went with him; and much people followed him, and thronged him.

And a certain woman, which had an issue of blood twelve years,

And had suffered many things of many physicians, and had spent all that she had, and was nothing bettered, but rather grew worse,

When she had heard of Jesus, came in the press behind, and touched his garment.

For she said, If I may touch but his clothes, I shall be whole.

And straightway the fountain of her blood was dried up; and she felt in her body that she was healed of that plague.

And Jesus, immediately knowing in himself that virtue had gone out of him, turned him about in the press, and said, Who touched my clothes?

And his disciples said unto him, Thou seest the multitude thronging thee, and sayest thou, Who touched me?

And he looked round about to see her that had done this thing.

But the woman fearing and trembling, knowing what was done in her, came and fell down before him, and told him all the truth. And he said unto her, Daughter, thy faith hath made thee whole; go in peace, and be whole of thy plague.

Mark 5:24-34

Now notice, this woman was being led by the Spirit of God. The Holy Spirit led this woman to press her way through the crowd and to reach out in faith and touch the Lord Jesus Christ because she said, **If I may touch but his clothes, I shall be whole.** For twelve years she had spent all of her money on doctors but still was not whole. But the Spirit of God led her to put action to her faith. I believe that the Spirit of God led her to plow her way through the crowd just to touch Him. The Spirit of God did that. She was led by the Spirit of God.

What does it mean to be led by the Spirit of God? To be led by the Spirit of God means victory for you in every case. When the Spirit of God leads you, you will show God faith.

Now look at verse 35: **While he yet spake, there came from the ruler of the synagogue's house certain which said, Thy daughter is dead: why troublest thou the Master any further?** Remember Jairus who came over and told Jesus to come and lay His hands on his daughter so she would be healed and live? Well, now she is dead.

I don't know if you are ready for this, but I am going to give it to you anyway: "So what?" Jesus is Truth. So what if she is dead? The spirit of death is the enemy of God! Romans 5:12 tells us that death entered into the world because of sin. Jesus never would accept death because when the Spirit of God is in you, you don't accept the works of hell. You only accept what the Bible says, and that is victory.

Be Not Afraid, Only Believe

Follow this closely — Look at verse 36: **As soon as Jesus heard the word that was spoken, he saith unto the ruler of the synagogue, Be not afraid, only believe.** Fear robs faith from you. The evil spirit of fear robs your faith because he pries and tortures the natural part of you. And if you don't know that **faith is the substance of things hoped for, the evidence of things not seen** (Heb. 11:1), then you will begin to lean towards the natural because faith isn't a part of you. And the moment that you do, you will be cut off from the supernatural. You will be cut off from God, and He won't be able to help you anymore. Is that clear? He can't help you anymore. The Bible says that the natural man understandeth not the things of God. (1 Cor. 2:14.) Not only does the natural part of you not know the will of God, it can't know. That is the reason that the devil digs and tortures you. He is trying to get you to lean over to the natural because if you ever do, you are whipped.

God is a faith God, and the Spirit of God will lead you to stand steadfast in faith, but the spirit of doubt and the spirit of fear will come and try to make you afraid that it won't happen. Notice what Jesus said to the ruler, the father of the child who is dead. He said, **Be not afraid, only believe** (Mark 5:36). Fear and faith don't mix. You need to resist the spirit of fear in order to walk forward in faith. You need to say, "In Jesus' name, I resist the spirit of fear. I command the spirit of fear to go from me."

So what did Jesus do? The Scriptures say,

> **And he suffered no man to follow him, save Peter, and James, and John the brother of James.**
>
> **And he cometh to the house of the ruler of the synagogue, and seeth the tumult, and them that wept and wailed greatly.**
>
> **Mark 5:37,38**

Now if your little girl had died, you and your relatives would be in a lot of turmoil too. Some of you would be passing out, and they would be bringing you to with camphor. Others would be crying and wailing, "Oh, God, why did this happen to me?" And it would take you six months to a year or two to get over it.

I know. I have been through it. I was ten years old when my mother died, and we thought you were supposed to mourn and cry and wring your hands and run and scream for a year. Every time I heard a sad song I would go and hide somewhere and cry for thirty minutes because it would remind me of my mother's death. It was the same way when my nineteen-year-old brother who played football in high school died.

You don't have to die at thirty-seven and leave behind your three small children. You don't have to die at nineteen. But we didn't know anything about God's healing power. We were attending a church that had blackboards with a sign over them that said, "Pray for the sick," and we put the sick people's names on the blackboards. The whole church would pray for their names, and they would all die. Writing names on a blackboard for healing isn't in the Bible, but laying hands on sick people in Jesus' name is. Anointing people with oil in the name of Jesus and taking authority over disease are in the Bible, but we didn't know, so they died.

Now sometimes you know what to do, but you don't have the victory in a particular area, and you have a hard time not doubting God. It was that way with me when my daughter backslid. My heart was completely broken and shattered into a thousand pieces, but I couldn't do anything about it. Then one day the Spirit of God fell upon me when I was in the car and told me what to do and where I had made my mistakes.

Now you would think that a guy like me who goes around the country teaching the Bible would have a little sense. But I will tell you right now, you don't have half as much sense as you think you do when you get in the Holy Presence of the Almighty God. In other words, when you get God's ideas on the subject, you will find out how much sense you really have, and you will be utterly amazed at how dumb you are. But you will never know how dumb you are until you get into the Holy Presence of God and He pulls the curtains away from you and lets you see exactly the way it is.

At the time, I had just come out of a meeting in San Antonio, Texas. When I had prayed for people, they had fallen all over the floor under the power of God, and God had healed them. Now three days later God is telling me, "You've been doubting Me. You've been wondering when I'm going to come and visit your daughter and bring her back into My family. And you've been wondering why I haven't hurried up and done it. Why don't you repent of your doubt and stand in faith, and I'll do it for you? Her faith could never get Me to visit her, but your faith could. Your faith is strong enough, but you're not applying your faith correctly. Instead, you're letting your mind come in and start wondering."

Sometimes you just need to grab your head and shake it and say, "Be quiet! Shut up!" My daughter needed that the night her angel appeared to her. I had to grab her and shake her because she was so scared that her teeth were rattling. If you had just floated in from a nightclub and your angel appeared to you, what would you do? When the Lord told me to repent of my doubt, put my faith to work, and He would visit her," He knew what He was doing. "Besides that," He said, "you haven't been loving your daughter like you should. That hasn't been My Spirit leading you to love your daughter that way."

When you check up on yourself, you would be surprised how many things you do that the Holy Spirit doesn't lead you to do. "Now," He said, "let Me lead you. When your daughter comes in, look at her and say, 'I love you, and Jesus loves you,' then shut up." The first night I tried to do that I had to make myself do it. I wanted to say what I had been saying, "Where have you been until two o'clock in the morning? I didn't raise you like that!" But the Lord said, "Shut up!" so I shut up.

You might think you have a right to say what you want to your child because you are their parent. You might think you have a right to go around and give your child orders and love your child any way you want to. I have news for you: you don't have the right. You have the Bible, and you have the Spirit of God, and that is all you have. God loves you, but it is *your* responsibility to believe what the Bible says so the Holy Spirit can lead you. You have to listen to what God says and do it. There is just no way around it.

Stand in Faith

Now where the average Christian misses it is right here — they act like Jairus' relatives and friends instead of like Jairus. Notice what Jairus does when his relatives and friends are in such a tumult. He keeps walking! "Didn't he hear what the messenger had told him earlier — **Thy daughter is dead: why troublest thou the Master any further?** (Mark 5:35) In other words, "What's the matter with you, Mister?" But instead of listening to the people or listening to the messenger, he listens to Jesus who said, **Be not afraid, only believe** (v. 36), and just keeps on walking toward the house.

Why? Because the father believed in Jesus' words and believed in the words that he, himself, had spoken earlier: **Come and lay thy hands on her, that she may be healed; and she shall live** (v. 23). He is applying his faith by using a doctrine of the Church, the laying on of hands, and believes that she will live.

Unfortunately most people will not stand steadfast in faith long enough for the great and mighty blessings of God to come upon them. I am not talking about just a few of them here, I am talking probably about ninety-eight percent of them. They just won't do it. And as a result, they miss out.

Now look again at the last four words that the father said in verse 23: **and she shall live.** Jesus said in Mark 11:23 that you can have whatsoever you say, and Jairus said, **and she shall live.** The father said that in faith about his daughter, **and she shall live.** Those are the last four words

he said, **and she shall live**. There are no maybe's about it.
Jesus said you can have whatever you say if you will only
believe, and the father said, **and she shall live**. She did, and
so can you.

4

Talk Heaven Talk

And [God] calleth those things which be not as though they were.

Romans 4:17

What is heaven talk? It is a language that looks defeat straight in the face and calls it victory. It is the language of heaven. It is the language that Jesus used when He told the relatives and friends of Jairus who were mourning at his house, **The damsel is not dead, but sleepeth** (Mark 5:39). But she was dead! But Jesus said she wasn't! But she was. But He said she wasn't.

Now that will jar the natural part of you. That will jar the human side of you, and you will come alive and automatically begin to say, "No, no, no, that isn't correct, Jesus! She is in there in her room. She has been dead for a long time — three or four hours. We sent a man to tell You so a long time ago. Didn't You get our message?"

What you have to understand here is that she was dead, but Jesus said she wasn't, but she was. This may sound confusing, but it really makes perfect sense because there are two languages being spoken in two different worlds here. One language is being spoken in the natural world — the world that you, I and the family live in. It is earthly language. In earthly language, she is dead. She has taken her last breath and isn't breathing anymore. The spirit of death has come and attacked her with some disease or affliction and has taken the life right out of her, and she is dead, speaking in earthly terms.

You might say, "Why did He say she was not dead when she was dead?" Jesus was being led by the Spirit of God to speak heaven words on earth, and there is no death in heaven.

Know Who You Are in Christ

Now when you are born again by the Spirit of God, you have a right to talk heaven talk, too. But just because you have a right to talk heaven talk is no guarantee that you will. Many Christians believe that they talk heaven talk because they are saved and Jesus rescued them, but they don't. Jesus blesses them because they are a child of God and worship Him and love Him. They work for Him, and He blesses them. But that is no sign that they talk heaven talk or will ever see a miracle as long as they live.

In order to see a miracle of God's power, you have to know who *you* are in Christ Jesus, and you have to learn a new language. That language is not tongues. You can't learn tongues. When you speak in tongues, you don't know what you are saying and neither does anybody else. God says,

> **For he that speaketh in an unknown tongue speaketh not unto men, but unto God: for no man understandeth him; howbeit in the spirit he speaketh mysteries.**
>
> **1 Corinthians 14:2**

He speaks in mysteries in the Spirit. Only the Holy Ghost can interpret what you say when you speak in other tongues. He knows what your spirit is saying, but nobody else does. Speaking in tongues is a gift and is in a language that you don't understand.

The new language I am talking about learning is a language that you can understand. It is a language that looks death and disease straight in the face and commands them to leave. It is a language that is based on God's Word.

42

Know the Spirit Through the Word

The Holy Spirit will help you. He is a Person. He is a Divine Personality sent from heaven to live inside you to teach you the ways of God and to lead you into all truth. He talks to your spirit through the Word of God. But if the Word of God is not in your spirit, how can He talk heaven talk to you? He can't! It is just as simple as that. He can't.

Some people think that because they are saved and baptized in the Holy Ghost that the Holy Ghost is going to lead them into victory. What the Holy Spirit is going to do is to lead you into the knowledge of the Word that you have put into your spirit. That is the way He is going to lead you. And if you have not taken the time yourself to put the Bible into your spirit, how can the Holy Spirit ever help you?

The Holy Spirit won't unfold to you about James 5:14,15 if you haven't read about it before. How can He? You haven't been taking the time to study it. As a result, you don't talk heaven talk, but I am telling you that God wants you to be led by the Spirit of God in everything. But the Spirit of God only leads through the knowledge of His Word.

Now you might say, "The Spirit of God doesn't ever come upon me and tell me to do anything." He doesn't because you don't know any Scripture. Do you understand that? You don't know much of the Word. How can He tell you if the Scriptures aren't in you — if you don't know them? How can He give you an order? You wouldn't even know what He was talking about.

But if you will take the time to learn who you are in Christ Jesus and will become a Bible reader and a Bible believer and will get those Scriptures in your spirit, then the Holy Ghost will speak to your spirit about those Scriptures. He will remind you who you are in Christ Jesus and what the Bible says.

That is the reason that God warns the Church not to have weak elders and deacons on their boards. Why? How can a weak man help somebody? God doesn't want leaders in the Church who aren't strong. God wants leaders who can walk in your front door when you are defeated and say, "No you don't, devil! Not to this family you don't!"

He doesn't want someone floating in from the church saying, "I just don't understand what happened here. Do you know? I don't." Someone like that needs to go home, get under the bed and stay there until they find out who they are in Christ Jesus! Church leaders like that are dangerous out in public.

God doesn't bless ignorance or weakness. He tells the strong to help the weak. The Bible says, He that is weak, let him say he is strong. (Joel 3:10.) Let him say it! Let him say it! Let him say it! You have to *say* you are strong even if you are weak. You have to recognize your weaknesses and start saying you are strong. You can do something about it! You have as much right as the next guy to do something. There is nobody in the world that God loves more than He loves you. But you will have to learn to talk heaven talk. The Spirit of God will only lead you to talk heaven talk. Do you understand that?

Stay Balanced

Did you ever hear somebody say, "I felt led of the Spirit to write seven checks, but I didn't have any money in the bank?" That wasn't the Spirit! That's not what the Word told them to do. That was their idea! You are supposed to have enough common sense to know how to look at your checkbook and figure out that you don't have any money in the bank. You aren't supposed to go around writing a bunch of checks with no money in the bank. Now God may cover one or two of them for you, but if you keep that up, He isn't going to cover them, and eventually you will get into a mess.

When I go to the penitentiaries, I talk to people like that. They say, "But I didn't mean to, Mister Hayes. I didn't mean to. If I had it to do over again, I wouldn't do that. What makes you think I would do that again?" Then I say, "Because you were stupid. You listened to the devil." Then they give me this dumbfounded look and say, "The devil! Who's the devil?" Unfortunately most people don't even know who the devil is!

Then there are the people who actually think they have a right to talk any way they want to and do whatever they want to. They go around saying, "I'm a Christian, and God will cover me. I belong to God, and I trust the Lord, so whatever I decide is probably what God would have decided anyway."

You and God may not end up deciding the same way. He wants you to believe the Bible and talk heaven talk and stop talking earth talk — except when you go to see your relatives. You have to talk a little earth talk with them just to be friendly. You might say something like, "How are you doing, Aunt Bessie? Do you have any coconut pie?" "Yes, I have some." "I'll take a piece, thank you." Now I love my relatives, but since I got baptized in the Holy Ghost and began to pray with other tongues and cast out devils and pray for the sick, just going to visit and talk natural earth talk can seem dull at times.

"Do you cast out devils, Brother Norvel?" "Yes, I do. Don't you?" Devils don't let your mind think straight, so you need to take authority over them and bind them up. Even though you are a Spirit-filled Christian, devils can still press in on your mind and not let you think straight. They make you look at what is happening in the natural realm. Who cares what is happening? If you don't like what is happening, call it the way you want it to be, and that is the way it will be. It will turn out just the opposite of the way the circumstances appear.

Call Those Things That Be Not

Look at what Romans 4:17,18 says Abraham did:

> **(As it is written, I have made thee a father of many nations,) before him whom he believed, even God, who quickeneth the dead, and calleth those things which be not as though they were.**
>
> **Who against hope believed in hope, that he might become the father of many nations, according to that which was spoken, So shall thy seed be.**

Abraham wanted a son, and God had promised him one, yet his wife had passed her child-bearing years. So he called it the way he wanted it to be, and he had a son. He walked around speaking in faith. And whether you know it or not, God made Abraham like unto God, and he is your father and my father. He is not your eternal Father. God is your eternal Father. But Abraham is your father of faith.

What Abraham did sounds just like what Jesus did when He saw Jairus' daughter. He stood right up in the face of defeat and confessed victory. He stood in the face of death and said, "No, I won't accept that. I say she lives. She is not dead." The Spirit of God was in Him and was leading Him to say that, but the people laughed Him to scorn because it sounded like foolishness. It was too different from what they had seen with their eyes. So they did not believe.

Because of their unbelief, Jesus puts them all out, then takes the father and the mother of the damsel and them that were with them and enters into the room where the damsel is lying. (Mark 5:40.) Verse 41 says that He took the damsel by the hand and said to her: **Damsel, I say unto thee, arise.** And she arose.

She lived because He refused to accept the spirit of death, and He dared to call those things which be not as though they are. You don't have to accept the things the devil gives to you; do you understand that? You don't have to. You have a right to call those things which be not as though they were.

If Jesus had not called those things that be not as though they were, He would have said, "Okay, she's dead. Let's bury her." If he had, then He would have agreed with the spirit of death, but the Bible tells us that the spirit of death is an enemy of God, and you know that Jesus is not going to agree with the devil. As a matter of fact, you can't find anywhere in the Bible that Jesus ever agrees with the devil. And if you have ever read the book of Revelation, you will know that the devil will ultimately be cast into the lake of fire and so will death. (Rev. 20:10,14.) They will be the last enemies to be destroyed, so He isn't about to agree with them.

Now the people outside who had laughed Jesus to scorn just moments before weren't laughing anymore. As a matter of fact, the Scriptures say:

> **And they were astonished with a great astonishment.**
> **And he charged them straitly that no man should know it; and commanded that something should be given her to eat.**
>
> **Mark 5:42,43**

Why didn't He want them to know it? Because they would kill Him! You won't have too many friends when you start obeying the Bible either. When you start speaking in new tongues and casting out devils and telling all of your friends about it, see how many you have left. Go ahead. Call them all up and tell them, "I cast out devils in Jesus' name." Brother, they won't be at your house Sunday for lunch. They really won't.

And it is too bad because it is all scriptural, and it is all beautiful. And your friends who don't understand don't know what they're missing.

Jesus wanted to live out His time like He was supposed to and die on the cross like He was supposed to so that you and I can walk around in peace and joy. He did it so that we can talk about a God Who loves us and talk about a God Who has more power than the devil and talk about a God Who sets our spirits free. And we are supposed to tell others because Jesus said to. But to some people it doesn't make any difference what Jesus said. To them it is what people think that makes a difference. You can't go by what people think! You have to go by what the Bible says.

Speak to Your Mountain

Awhile back, a woman walked up to me all mad and shook up in a convention where I was speaking and said, "Mr. Hayes!" I said, "Yes, ma'am." She said, "I don't believe what you teach!" I said, "Well, I'm sorry you don't believe the Bible, ma'am." She said, "I believe the Bible!" I said, "Oh, but you don't believe what I teach?" "That's right, I don't believe what you teach because it doesn't work," she said.

Then I said, "What did I say that wasn't chapter and verse?" "Well," she said, "I don't know, but what you say doesn't work. My husband got cancer when he was forty-one years old, and he died. But he believed that the Lord was going to heal him right up until the last breath. All of our Spirit-filled Christian friends prayed for him, but he died anyway. It just doesn't work."

About that time, the Spirit of God said to me, "Minister Mark 11:23 to her. He didn't obey that." So I said, "Let me ask you a question. Did your husband ever talk to the cancer?" And she said, "No, I never did hear him holding a conversation with the cancer."

I said, "Well, Mark 11:23 says that *whosoever* shall say unto this mountain, **Be thou removed, and be thou cast into the sea; and shall not doubt in his heart, but shall**

believe, it will done for him. Is your husband included in the *whosoever*?" And she said, "Well, yes." Then I asked her, "Did you ever hear your husband saying, `Cancer, you can't kill me. Cancer, get out of my body. Cancer, go from me in Jesus' name. I command you to go from me in Jesus' name. Cancer, I'm not giving you any choice. I said go from me in Jesus' name.'"

Always remember, if you give cancer a choice, it will kill you. And that man, who died with cancer, gave cancer a choice. My mother, my own flesh and blood mother, died with cancer at the age of thirty-seven, but she gave cancer a choice waiting to see if God was going to do anything about it or not.

The Bible has already been spoken out of the mouth of God, and the Bible has already been written. God isn't going to do anymore. God does for you what you do. All the time and every time, God does what you do, and He will do it for anybody. When Jesus said "whosoever," that is exactly what He meant, "whosoever." If you don't want something, come against it in Jesus' name and tell it to get out, and it will leave you.

I said, "Read it for yourself, ma'am, and study it." Then she said, "Do you mean to tell me that my husband was one verse of Scripture away from life, and if he had obeyed this, he could have lived and not died?" "That's exactly what I'm telling you," I said, "since healing can be just one verse of Scripture away."

What you have to understand is that every doctor in the hospital can say you are going to die with that disease, and they are telling you the truth because they are speaking from the natural. But I am telling you that you are only one verse of Scripture away from perfect health — just one verse!

That one verse can cause God's power to come into your body and drive out all affliction. That one verse has to come out of you, and you have to claim it for yourself. It has to be in your spirit like your right arm is a part of your body. That one verse of Scripture has to be in your spirit, just that strong. But it will never become a part of you unless you are willing to study it, memorize it and confess it hundreds and hundreds of times because **faith cometh by hearing, and hearing by the word of God** (Rom. 10:17). And if you don't hear yourself say it, it will never become a part of you, not to the point that it will work for you.

You might say, "I haven't studied the healing verses in the Bible or memorized them yet, but I know they're in there." Then you had better start. Smith Wigglesworth, a twentieth century apostle of faith, said that if you wait until you get sick to believe God for your healing, then you have waited too long because you are supposed to get the Scripture in you when you are well. Then when the devil comes and knocks you in the bed, you aren't trying to believe God in this area for the first time.

You Can Change Your Circumstances

So what are you waiting for? Speak to your mountain and call those things that be not as though they were. You have a God-given right since you have been born again by the Spirit of God and the third person of the Trinity lives in you. So why don't you decide, right now, what you want to change. The Holy Spirit will never help you change the situation until you make up your mind that you will look straight at it and call it different. But until you come to that place, the Holy Spirit will never help you, never.

Now, whatever you want to change, call it different with your mouth. If your husband has a stinking attitude, call him sweet. If your children sass you, start confessing, "My children are sweet and nice." Remember, the Spirit of God lives in you, and you must confess victory so He can work for you.

If your body is weak, call yourself strong. If you feel like you have not been loving Jesus enough or worshipping Jesus enough, start saying, "I love You, Jesus. I worship You, Jesus." Start confessing the thing that you were not doing before so you can get it on the inside of your spirit and make it a part of you. If your body is sick, don't call it sick. Call it healed. The Bible says, **Let the weak say, I am strong** (Joel 3:10). Don't say it two or three or four or five times a week then stop. Say it over and over again, a hundred times, two hundred times, three or four hundred times until it becomes a part of you.

If you will listen to the Spirit of God, He will lead you that way every day. Listen to Him, and be led by the Spirit of God in your confession. If you decide not to listen to the Spirit of God, I'm going to tell you right now what you are going to say every day — nothing much. That is you being led by you.

To follow the Holy Spirit, you have to make up your mind that you are going to obey God instead of yourself. It isn't what you want to do that matters. Who cares what you want to do? Do what God wants you to do. He wants you to quote the Scriptures so He can perform them for you. So why wait?

5

Cast Out Devils and Heal the Sick!

And [Jesus] gave them power and authority over all devils, and to cure diseases.

Luke 9:1

Devils cause all the harm on earth, and you have power over all of them. But if *you* don't *know* that *you have power over them*, then they won't even listen to you. You have to *know* who you are and *stand* in your authority in Christ Jesus. Luke 9:1 is a verse that will get all of the weakness out of you: **Then he called his twelve disciples together, and gave them power and authority over all devils, and to cure diseases.**

All you have to do is know your authority in Him and say, "In Jesus' name, devils and disease, get out! Get out of this room! In Jesus' name, get out! I belong to God, so go from me!" Some people may say, "Brother Norvel, I can't do it that way." Yes, they can if they will pray for a holy boldness. The Holy Ghost will help them. But they have to pray for holy boldness so they have no shame in them. Many times what robs Christians, God's family, is the natural pride they have in them. We can't have any pride when it comes to obeying the Gospel.

Heal the Sick

Let me give you an example of how the Spirit of God led me to heal the sick awhile back. I was on my way home from a Full Gospel Businessmen's convention when I stopped at a convenience store in Nashville, Tennessee. I

53

was looking around the counters waiting to fill my car up with gas when the Spirit of God drew my attention to this lady. She looked like she was about twenty-eight years of age. So I went up to her and said, "Young lady, let me ask you a question. Are you in pain?" "Yes, sir," she said, "I have a migraine headache. Sometimes I even beat my head against the wall. When they last for seven or eight days, they nearly kill me. This one has been with me now for quite a while."

I said, "You will never have one again after we pray." Then I asked her if she and her husband would like to step inside my motor home so we could pray. Once we went in the motor home, I just put my hands on her head and said, "I break your power, Satan, in Jesus' name." All of a sudden, the power of God hit her, and she began to weep. She sobbed and sobbed. Then the Holy Ghost brought her complete victory, and I knew it. So I said, "She's healed. She's well." Then I just backed off and began to thank the Lord.

She sat there saturated in the love of God and the peace of God, and she wept and wept. Finally I said, "You're free now. You're free." After a while she could get enough breath to talk and said, "That's right. I'm free. It's all gone. I'm free."

Then I looked over at her husband and said, "You could do that if you'd pay the price to do it. You could see miracles, deliverances, and crooked legs straightened. But they don't come cheap. Do you understand that? God's got a test you're going to have to pass." "What test is that?" he asked. "Abraham's test," I said, "No more and no less. God made Abraham like unto Himself, and God made Abraham my father and your father of faith. So your faith has to be like Abraham's faith — no more and no less." I talked about Romans 4:17.

If only I could have met her eight years ago, all the pain and agony she has been going through could have been over with by now. But she has been putting up with it around Christian people for all of those years. My brother or sister, when the Spirit of God comes upon you and gives you an order, He needs to know that you won't give up. The Spirit of God would not have even dealt with me to pray for that woman in the store if He hadn't known that I wouldn't give up until that spirit was broken. He knew that I would just keep on and on and on until it was broken. I had intended to stay there until that old foul spirit that had been around her for eight years causing headaches left. He knew I would just stand over them and say, "No you don't, devil, in Jesus' name. No you don't. No you don't."

You just have to make up your mind and say, "No," to the devil. The Spirit of God always leads you to say to the devil, "No!" Every time you come upon something that is going to cause you harm and defeat, open up your mouth and say, "Devil, no!" Don't ever look at the situation and start wondering. That will only lead you into a bunch of confusion, and you won't even know who you are or if God did it or the devil did it. Remember, whenever anything doesn't bring joy, peace, power or love, say, "No!" and you will *stay* free because the Word makes you free.

Cast Out Devils

I don't know if you know it or not, but if you haven't found out, I will let you in on a little information. You can't hide from God. Sometimes people think, "I'm just going to catch a plane and go out somewhere and get away from everything." I have news for you. I don't care if you go to Africa and get behind a bush, God will be right on the other side of bush looking at you, saying, "What are you doing here? I still want you to cast out devils." And you will say, "Oh, not me, Lord, not me. I'm just a nice housewife, Lord. I'm just a nice fellow, Lord. I just want to be a decent citizen." I used to tell Him that. I would say, "Lord, just let me be a good member of my church. I want to be a businessman. I just want to be a nice fellow, Lord. I don't want to get involved with these goofed up people. Don't let me get involved with them, Lord. I just want to be a nice fellow."

One time it happened to me — He said, "Son, I want you to cast out devils." I said, "Ah, listen, Lord, my church never taught me to cast out devils." I thought if I told Him I was going to church, and He knew that I hadn't learned that in church that He would let me off the hook. But have I got news for you! God doesn't go by what a church does or doesn't do, especially when the church doesn't do all the doctrines of the New Testament church. He goes by the Bible!

So I said, "God, I don't know how to cast out devils. They never taught me that at church." When I said that, he said to me in no uncertain terms, "The sixteenth chapter of the book of Saint Mark teaches you!" I said, "Oh, yeah." Then He reminded me, "And you read it and studied it last week!" I said, "Oh, yes, Lord, yes. I do remember."

But He didn't stop there, and He said, "Well, now that you know, go up and cast the devil out of that girl." I said, "Oh, Lord, I've got friends here. And besides that, what if I try to cast the devil out, and it doesn't go? I would really be embarrassed, Lord." The people in the church I went to have a lot of pride. I didn't want to go up there and try to cast the devil out of somebody because of my pride.

But I wound up going, and I was going under the power of God. And I wound up casting the devil out of the girl. And it left, and God's power fell all over the place. The people in the church wound up shouting all over everywhere, and I got forty-five hugs and a few kisses.

Why? Because I did what God said to do and cast out the devil. Now I'm telling you something else, when you cast the devil out of somebody, they will love you for the rest of their life. They really will. In fact, the Lord told me one time, "You have to watch some people, son, because if you cast the devil out of them, they will love you too much." He said, "They will grab you and start kissing you all over your face, and you will have to use wisdom." So I said, "Yes, Sir," and I have watched it ever since.

On another occasion, God gave me an order for a really desperate situation. At that time, Lester Sumrall, who has cast out a lot of devils, and I were holding a meeting in Chattanooga, Tennessee, at the Y.M.C.A. in one of the ballrooms. One day I looked up, and a hippie came walking in with long hair and a beard wearing moccasins and a sleeveless shirt. Two black bags were hanging from his arms, and he had an Indian headband around his head and a tooth hanging around his neck.

He came walking up the stairs and said, "Something has been playing tricks on my mind." I said, "Yeah, I'll buy that." "Something told me to come in here," he said. "Yeah, that's right, too," I said. Dr. Sumrall was standing right beside me when I said, "Let us pray for you." So we just took him by the hand and started to say, "In Jesus' name, come out of him! In Jesus' name, come out of him!"

The moment we began to do that he broke and began to cry. When we turned his hands loose, he just stood there weeping and trembling, saying, "I didn't know God loved me. I didn't know God loved me. I didn't know God was real." He ended up appearing on TV and in the papers. When that happened, I extended the meeting even after Dr. Sumrall left and started a youth revival. So many people got saved that we had to buy a house in order to continue the ministry.

As it turned out, Frank, the one who had just been saved, had been on his way to Florida to get a load of acid to sell to the hippies at the hippie house he ran in Nashville, Tennessee, when his car broke down. He wasn't far from our meeting, so he decided to come. He never did go back to Nashville. He said that he had never found anything like this in his life and that they could just take the hippie house and do whatever they wanted to with it.

After a while we put him about half in charge of the house. Of course, we had another man to oversee it and so forth because Frank was new in the Lord, but he had a lot of common sense and was able to help people who would come out to the house and had been on dope.

Trust the Leading of Your Spirit

One day, however, I was just riding in my car through a shopping center in Cleveland, Tennessee, when the Spirit of God fell on me, and the Lord said to me, "Go to Chattanooga, to that house." So I took off towards Chattanooga.

As I rounded the curve in the winding driveway going up to the house, I saw Frank at the front door. All of the sudden, the front door flew open at the house, and Frank came running out to my car, saying, "Oh, Brother Norvel, the Lord sent you here! The Lord sent you here!" I said, "I know He did! I know He did! The Spirit of God told me to come here."

Then he went on, "There's a boy upstairs who has lost his mind. He doesn't even know his own name. He's a real padded cell case. They brought him here from his college, and his psychiatrist even came with him. They said they had seen me on television and that I had said that Norvel Hayes and Lester Sumrall had cast the devils out of me!"

So I walked upstairs, and they introduced me to the college psychiatrist, and he said, "A year ago I didn't even believe in this kind of stuff, but I started listening to some tapes, and I started wondering if there could be some truth to it. Then one day I was watching television, and I saw this fellow on television, and he said that Lester Sumrall and Norvel Hayes had cast the devils out of him.

"I knew then that the devils must have been in this client of mine because he had taken off all of his clothes to go march with some people down the street when his mind snapped. Now he doesn't even know his own name. We've called his daddy who lives in New Jersey to come down here and pick him up, but he won't be here until tomorrow. So when I saw this on TV, I got permission from his college to bring him over here. Would you be willing to pray for him?"

"I will if you'll leave me alone," I said. He looked at me kind of funny, then I said, "Do you know anything about casting out devils or deliverance?" "Oh, no, I don't know anything about it. I didn't even believe in it a year ago, but I believe it's real now," he said. "Oh, it's real all right," I said, "Devils will drive you crazy. They will get into your mind and turn you into another creature. If it's a thieving spirit, you'll become a thief. If it's a lustful spirit, you'll commit adultery. If it's a lesbian spirit, you'll become a lesbian. If it's a cursing spirit, you'll curse God. But it all depends on what kind of a spirit it is and if it gets in you. If it does, you will become whatever that spirit is, but you will have to resist it in Jesus' name. The Bible says when you resist the devil, he will flee from you. (James 4:7.) *Flee* means, 'run away or escape from danger'.[1] Glory be to God, they will run from you. But unless you resist them, they won't run from you."

When I finished talking, the boy was still sitting there, and I asked everyone to leave the room and leave us alone. That isn't much different than what Jesus did in Luke 8:54. Notice what it says here, **And he put them all out.** Look at what he did: He put them all out, unbelief and all. Verses 55 and 56 say:

---

[1] *Webster's New World Dictionary*, 2d ed., s.v. "flee."

59

And he put them all out, and took her by the hand, and called, saying, Maid, arise.

And her spirit came again, and she arose straightway: and he commanded to give her meat.

And her parents were astonished: but he charged them that they should tell no man what was done.

He said not to tell anyone because it wasn't time for Him to die yet on the cross. If people had found out He was doing things like that, the old religious spirit in them would have killed Him.

The same thing happens today. If you walk into a house where the family has never been taught about God's miracle-working power and tell one of their relatives who is dying, "Jesus wants to heal you right now," that old religious spirit will rise up in them and say, "Well, this is what we believe. In our church, we, we, we . . . ." Who cares about what your church believes or what your relatives think? It is what the Bible says that counts!

So I began to pray for the boy. I went over to him and put my hands on him said, "In Jesus' name, come out of him! You can't have his mind because I say you can't. I'm not going to let you have it. I know you want it devil, but I'm telling you that the One inside of me is greater than you, and I'm telling you in no uncertain terms to come out of him in Jesus' name. Let his mind go free. I'm not giving you any choice, Satan. The Holy Spirit of God came upon me in Cleveland, Tennessee, in a shopping center and gave me an order to come here and cast you out. I've come here to cast you out, and I'm not taking no for an answer. Come out of him in Jesus' name. I said come out of him."

For seven and a half hours I did that. I'd go over and rest a while, then I would get back up and walk over to him again. Finally he got up and stood on one foot, and white foam began to run out of his mouth down to the floor, and his mind snapped back into him. Do you understand me? His mind snapped back into him!

How To Stay Free

Well, the next day the father came to get the boy, and they wanted me to talk to him, so I said, "Mister, you're going to take this boy back to New Jersey, and he is in his right mind. It took seven and a half hours of praying by faith with authority for God to come and give him his mind back. He is normal now, and he can talk to you and hold a conversation with you. Last night he couldn't even do that. He didn't even know his own name. All he could say was, 'Nah, nah, nah!' He was a padded cell case who had to have somebody with him at all times."

Then I asked his father, "What kind of church do you go to, sir?" He said, "I go to a Bible-believing church." I said, "They all say they believe the Bible, but they really don't. Most of them believe part of it but not all of it."

Since I know that the Bible says that the devils will try to come back, I wanted to make sure his father would take him to a church where the people knew how to resist the devil, so I said, "If his mind starts getting confused at all, do you have a church where this young man can walk down front to the altar and ask the pastor to lay his hands on him and take authority, in Jesus' name, over the confusion?"

Then he said, "I don't think my pastor knows anything about what you're talking about." Then I warned him, saying, "Mister, you had better find a Bible-believing, New Testament church where they believe in the doctrine of laying on of hands. It's in the Bible, you know." When he asked me what he should look for, I gave him the names of some of the Full Gospel Churches that I knew about and told him to make sure that the pastor believed in the ministry of laying on of hands.

"Keep your son at the altar," I told him, "until he gets strong and gets the Word of God on the inside of him. Don't let him miss a service. Get him in church and make him a part of his church. Let the elders of the church and the pastor lay hands on him, and let God's power go right down through him in Jesus' name."

A few days later, the psychiatrist called me in my office in Cleveland, Tennessee and said, "Mr. Hayes, the college president would like you to have lunch with him someday, if you can. He wants to talk with you." I said to myself, "This is going to be good. I believe I'll go." And I went.

When I arrived, the psychiatrist, the president and one of his assistants invited me to sit down with them for dinner. While we were eating, the president looked up at me and said, "Mr. Hayes, I appreciate you praying for that boy and getting him free. That was something else. Now I have a question to ask you. Would you pray to God that He would bless this school and bless this college and bless this staff so that we could be led by Him and know the truth? I know this campus needs a blessing, and as president of this college, I would like you to do it in my office."

So as soon as we finished dinner, we all went into his office and held hands and prayed the blessings of God down upon the school in Jesus' name.

Know Your Power and Authority in Christ

Now it was the Spirit of God Who led me in each of these situations. *But know this: the Spirit of God wouldn't have led me to do these things unless He had known that I would do them, and He only led me according to the knowledge of the Bible that I already knew.* Now He won't lead you according to what I know or what your neighbor knows, but He will lead you according to what *you* know.

If you want to do something *for* God, then learn something *about* God. You might say, "Well, I know God, Brother Norvel." But do you know your authority in Christ Jesus? Do you know the ninth chapter of the book of Luke?

Do you know that God has given you authority and power over *all* devils and to cure *all* diseases? If you didn't before you started reading this chapter, you should know now that power is available to you.

6
Go Win Souls!

Go ye into all the world, and preach the gospel to every creature.

Mark 16:15

Do you know that a national survey claims that ninety-five percent of born-again Christians have never won a soul to Christ. Did you ever stop and think about that? If you never did, think about it. You would probably be surprised to know how many people out there in the world want to know God but don't know how to know Him.

"Go Ye" Means "Go You!"

In Mark 16:15, Jesus said, **Go ye into all the world, and preach the gospel to every creature.** Now don't say, "Oh, He doesn't mean me. I just want to be nice to me and my four and no more. I just want to go to church on Sunday morning and go back home and have lunch, then go to sleep and do the same thing next Sunday. I'm not going to bring anybody to church with me, cast out devils or pray for the sick. God has ministers who will do all of that."

Dear Lord, that is what the devil tells people — Christian people! See the devil will always tell you, "That verse doesn't mean me." Well, you believe in God, don't you? Then,

> **Go ye into all the world, and preach the gospel to every creature.**
>
> **He that believeth and is baptized shall be saved; but he that believeth not shall be damned.**

Mark 16:15,16

Look again at what verse 16 says. If you don't believe in Jesus, you will be damned — damned forever. He that believes in Him and gives his life to Him shall be saved. But you say, "Well, I believe in Him, but I do what I want to do." Listen, that isn't believing in Him. You don't believe in Him. You believe in yourself, and you believe in the devil. You don't believe in God.

The Lord says in First John 1:6 that if a man stands up and says that he loves the Lord and then goes out and lives the way he wants to in the world, then he is a liar, and the truth isn't in him. Now you can live in just exactly what this world has to offer you if you want to. You can have a job, a career and friends. You can have barbecues, spend your Saturdays at the golf course and attending operas. You can live in that if you want to. You can have everything the world has to offer, and it will be exciting for a little while. But when you die, you will just go to hell. You won't go to heaven because you don't really belong to Jesus. You belong to the world, not to God.

But if you so choose to walk and live in the precious life, life here will be a lot more exciting to you, and when you die, you can go to heaven and live for all eternity in God's presence. As far as I am concerned, there is nothing worth losing heaven over. I was there once, and I am telling you now that you don't want to miss it. I didn't get to see very much of heaven, but the part I did see had tiny children in it who had died at an early age. They must have been anywhere from two days old to six years old and were staying in little rooms where the angels were teaching them till their little spirits grew up.

See, heaven is a real world. It isn't some spooky place out there in the sky somewhere where you just float around in the clouds with a bunch of spooky spirits wondering what your are doing there. No! That isn't what heaven is like. Heaven is a real world. It is just about like this world, only about ten times as beautiful. The grass is about ten times as green. The flowers are about ten times as pretty, and they don't have any bees to sting you. The air is saturated with peace and love, just saturated. Every ounce of you, from the top of your head to the bottom of your feet, your jaws, your eyes, every part of you is just saturated with the love of God. You couldn't even hate there if you wanted to.

It isn't like here where every now and then you have a blue Monday, and nothing seems to go right. God doesn't have any blue Mondays. With God, you stay on top of the mountain saturated with peace and love. In heaven there is no such thing as a blue Monday. In heaven there is no such thing as one sad moment because you are at the height of love, and you walk in it every day. Talk about beautiful, this is a place you wouldn't want to miss!

Give Your Life, Not Just Your Heart

So what do you need to do? Give your life to God instead of just your heart. There is a difference, you know. When you get born again by the Spirit of God, you give Jesus your heart. You are tired and sick of living in sin, and you want to have a relationship with Him. So when you go and repent before God, He forgives you of your sins and washes them all away. The confusion stops, and you begin to experience peace with Him.

You will remain in this state as long as you live your life clean and stay out of sin. But once you begin to commit sin again, then you will lose that precious walk you have with Him and go back into the natural again. Sin causes a person to live in the natural and to experience only what this world has to offer.

But if you give your life to God as well as your heart, then you make yourself available to take orders from God because your life belongs to Him. God doesn't need your ability. He needs your availability. If you aren't available to the Holy Spirit, then He can't use you. He will bless you to a degree because you know Him, but as far as giving you orders to go do something for Him are concerned, He can't. He can't because your life doesn't really *belong* to Him. Your heart belongs to Him, but not your life. You must be available. Remember, God will use anybody. He will use you. He will use me.

Personally I couldn't believe that God would call me to teach the Bible! I was a businessman. When He called me, I said, "God, are you sure you haven't made a mistake? What do You want me for? Besides, I don't really want to do that, Lord. I just want to be a nice businessman and citizen. I want to go to church on Sunday morning and be nice, Lord. I don't want to get involved with strange people and be casting out devils and all that stuff. I just want to be a nice fellow. I want to be a respected, successful businessman in the community. That is who I want to be."

But God had a different plan in mind and said, "I want you to cast out devils." Again I objected, "Lord, I was in a church that didn't teach me to cast out devils." Then He said, "The sixteenth chapter of the book of Saint Mark teaches you. You can read, can't you?" Have you ever had God ask you if you could read?

So I turned to Mark 16:17 and sure enough it says, **And these signs shall follow them that believe; In my name shall they cast out devils.** Now I knew the Lord wanted me to cast out devils. Now get ready for this. He wants you to cast them out too! This Scripture isn't for special, called out people. It is for *all* believers.

Fulfill the Whole Commission

You might say, "Well, I don't want to get involved in that kind of stuff. I just want to go to church on Sunday, have a good time and stay sweet." But that isn't what God said in verse 17. He said, **And these signs shall follow them that believe; in my name they shall cast out devils;**

they shall speak with new tongues. Have you received your power language yet? If you haven't, you need it real bad, and after you get it, you need to use it all the time. Why should you pray in your prayer language all of the time? Because it will help to keep you built up in God and won't allow the Gospel inside of you to become a stale, everyday thing. It will keep it fresh and new for you all the time, everyday.

Listen, I can hardly wait to get to church to see what is going to happen. I can hardly wait to see how the Spirit of God is going to move because you never can tell. I can hardly wait until Jesus speaks to me again Himself and tells me He loves me. I already know He loves me, but when He tells me I can hardly stand it.

One time Jesus told me to go up to a girl in the community that everybody thought was wrecked and cast the devil out of her because He loved her. This girl was worse than a street walker, but when the devil left her, the Lord sent her a boy to get married to, and she told her family, "I want you all to call Brother Norvel and ask him if he will stand beside the preacher at the wedding and read the Bible to me before the preacher performs the wedding ceremony."

So the family called me and asked me if I would do it. And I said, "Sure." So here I was at this wedding ceremony standing next to the pastor when she came walking down the isle. Just a few weeks before that she was worse than any street walker I had ever known.

While I was standing there with my Bible, Jesus spoke to me and said, "Son, I want to thank you for casting the devil out of this girl. Now she walks before you as an angel sent from heaven, clean and white as snow. She stands and walks before Me today as though she'd never sinned. Because I don't have any memory of the sins that she has committed, she walks toward you today as an angel." And then He thanked me for obeying the sixteenth chapter of the book of Saint Mark.

But you have to learn to be led by the Spirit of God. The Spirit of God will always lead you to obey the Scriptures. That is what the Spirit of God does. You may as well get ready because if your life belongs to God, He is going to lead you by the Holy Spirit in line with the Scriptures to obey them and to minister them to others.

It isn't good enough to stand back and say, "Oh, I don't want to do that, Lord." He will say to you, "The sixteenth chapter of the book of Saint Mark wants you to do it."

In my name they shall cast out devils; they shall speak with new tongues;

They shall take up serpents; and if they drink any deadly thing, it shall not hurt them; they shall lay hands on the sick, and they shall recover.

Mark 16:17,18

There is no reason for you to be sick. All you have to do is have hands laid upon you. Is that the only way that God heals? No, it isn't the only way, but it is one way. There are about seven or eight different ways that are mentioned in the Bible. And God can use any one of them.

Now, notice verses 19,20:

So then after the Lord had spoken unto them, he was received up into heaven, and sat on the right hand of God.

And they went forth, and preached every where, the Lord working with them, and confirming the word with signs following.

Jesus always confirms the Bible with signs following if He can ever get you to go forth and speak the Gospel out of your mouth.

Go Where He Sends You

Now go with me back to verse 15: **Go ye into all the world, and preach the gospel to every creature.** Are you open to do that? If you are, the Lord will send you somewhere. It may be down the street, but it may not be down the street either. It may be to some other town. It may be to some other country. But if you are available, the Lord will send you.

I have a friend that I have known for many years. When she was seventeen years old, she was praying and God told her, "I want you to go hold a meeting in a certain city and build a church for me." Do you believe God could use a seventeen-year-old girl, a teenager? Now if you were seventeen years old and God spoke to you and told you to go to a certain city and preach and build a church for Him and you don't have any money, what would you do? If you said, "I don't much believe I'd go." That answer could cause thousands of people to go to hell, and it would be your fault. But if Jesus speaks to you and tells you to do that, you had better obey Him!

Remember, Jesus has never made anybody's face like yours. Did you ever stop to think about that? He has never made anybody's mouth like yours. Jesus has never made another human being that talks like you do. He has never made two personalities alike, and He isn't going to either. The place He has for you nobody else can fill because they aren't you. It is a place that only you can fill.

You can reach people that I can't reach because of who you are. You know just how to flow with them, and God can give you the words to reach these particular people. You're not supposed to have the attitude that you love some people and don't love others. Some people say, "Did you ever meet somebody that you just didn't like?" I used to all the time, but I don't anymore because I have been set free from that kind of junk. I have learned to love everybody regardless of who they are or where they are from. Now that doesn't mean you have to live with them, but you do have to love them and try to win them to God if they will let you. If they won't let you, then you will just have to walk off.

So God told this seventeen-year-old girl to go to a certain city and preach for Him. You might say, "I don't believe in women preachers." Well, so what! Who cares what you believe? I was raised in a church where nobody believed in women preachers.

After you get baptized in the Holy Ghost and start praying in the Spirit and start seeing things in the Spirit world, you find out quickly that God is God and that God will do anything He wants to do, and He doesn't have to ask you or anyone else. Because God is God, He does what He wants to do.

So this seventeen-year-old girl told her mother, "Mother, I'm going to have to go to a certain city in Louisiana and preach because God told me to go preach and build a church for Him in that city." She said, "I know it, honey. I was just waiting for God to tell you because He already told me." Now she is a praying mother, and she doesn't have any money either, but she decides to go with her daughter, to back her up, to pray and to help her with the work.

Neither of them has any money, but they go anyway and find a lot just outside of town which is owned by a rich man. The mother and seventeen-year-old girl walk up to the man, and the girl says, "I was praying in my home town, and Jesus spoke to me and told me to come here and hold a meeting. Then I'm going to build a church here in town, but I need a lot. Can I use your lot?"

Since he was a wealthy businessman in town, he said, "Why not?" If I owned a big lot and a seventeen-year-old girl walked up to me and said, "God told me to come here and preach. Can I use your lot?" I would say, "Sure, if you're that wild, I'll let you have it. Go ahead and do it."

So they go out to pull up weeds because they don't even have enough money to buy a sickle. While she and her mother are pulling up weeds, an Assembly of God pastor passes by and asks, "What are you ladies doing?" The seventeen-year-old girl answers, "We're pulling up weeds so we can put some seats down here, and I can start preaching." "You?" he questions. "That's right — me," she says.

Then she goes on to ask him if he knows where she can get a piano. At first, he says, "No, I don't know where you can get one." Then she asks him, "You have one in your church, don't you?" He says, "Yes." Then she says, "Well, I would have one if you would loan it to me." He stalls around for a while then says, "Well, I can't loan you a piano out of our church because the dew would fall on it, and it would ruin it. If you had some kind of a shed out here to put it under, I'd be glad to loan it to you."

"Well, I'd have one if you'd build me one," she says. A nervy little thing, wasn't she? But sometimes we have not because we ask not. (James 4:2.) If you want something, you are simply going to have to speak up. Of course, by this time, he is wondering, "How did I ever get involved in this? What made me stop here?"

"Well," he said, "I do have two or three men in the church who are carpenters. They could probably build you a little shed somewhere." "They won't ever do it unless you ask them," she continued. "All right, I'll go ask them."

So they built a shed, and she got the piano, started a meeting, put out a few seats and six or eight people showed up the first night. She stood up there and preached to them. The next night, eight or ten showed up, and she preached to them. Then twelve or fifteen showed up, and she preached to them.

One night a family came in, and when she finished, they came down front to give their lives to Jesus. They were trembling, crying and weeping before God and had a little boy with them named Jimmy. He was an itty, bitty boy. One time during a meeting, he ran around all during that meeting, saying, "I'm going to be a preacher like that girl. I'm going to be a preacher." And sure enough, he became a well-known preacher. Thousands upon thousands of people have been saved under his ministry. Now you can see why God would speak to a seventeen-year-old girl and send her to an open field to preach.

Are You Willing To Knock on Doors?

Maybe you don't feel called to preach, but did you ever think about knocking on somebody's door to tell them about Jesus? Maybe you have and you had somebody come to the door and say gruffly, "Yes, what do you want!"

Then you said, "I want to talk to you about Jesus."

"Well, I don't want to talk about Jesus! I don't even believe in Him! Why should I want to talk about Him?"

About that time, the devil tells you, "This sure isn't your ministry," and then you act like a whipped pup and go back home. Don't act like a whipped dog and go back home. Just keep knocking on doors. Just keep on going.

Why, it wouldn't be long until you knock on somebody's door, and they will say, "Come on in! God knows we need something around here. Tell me, how do you get saved? He has done something for you, but why would He do something for me?"

Is there a door you have walked up to? Can you think of the person who would come to the door and say, "I'm so glad to see you. Had it not been for you, I'd be on my way to hell right now. But you came to my house and witnessed to me and won me to Jesus. You sat down with me and talked with me. You showed me what the Bible says, and now I'm saved. Praise God! You're the reason I'm going to heaven." Can you name the name of one soul who is on their way to heaven and not hell because of you?

Are You Willing To Pass Out Tracts?

Recently I received a letter from one of the girls on the Campus Challenge teams, and this is what she said:

Dear Brother Norvel,

I want to thank God, first of all, for leading you into this campus ministry so that people like me would have a chance to give out a book to a sinner or give out a tract to a sinner because on these campuses, these young people, boys and girls, are so possessed with the devil, and they need Jesus so bad.

I pray for them, and I consider it a great privilege for me to have the opportunity to even give out a tract or a book to a sinner young person so that I could have a part in winning their soul.

And I want to thank you for listening to the Lord about starting this ministry so that young people like me could have a part and be blessed in it. And I want to thank you and thank the Lord for the financial blessing that he has brought upon me that I never dreamed could ever be mine. Now I can buy new dresses and things of my own.

My brother or sister, let me tell you something. If you have an opportunity to go give a book or a tract out to somebody, go ahead and take that opportunity to do it. This girl did, and she is being blessed because of it.

Do you know that a national survey says that sixty-five percent of people who have come in contact with Jesus first came in contact with Him through a book or a tract? If you had asked me what I thought before I read this survey, I probably would have said fifteen percent. But this national survey said that sixty-five percent of born-again Christians first became interested in God through a book or tract that somebody gave them about the Lord Jesus Christ. Now stop and think about that — sixty-five percent!

Three or four years ago, I bought several cases of Christian funny books and just gave them away. One girl took one of those funny books to her sorority house at a university in New York. A year later, another girl walked up to her and asked, "Are you the girl who gives funny books and little books away to fraternities and sororities?" And she said, "That's me." Then the girl went on to tell how one of those funny books had landed on the coffee table at her sorority house and how one of the girls in the house read the funny book and got saved.

She gave her life to Jesus through that funny book, then the Spirit of God came upon her, and she began to witness to the rest of us. Since that time, six of us in that house have been saved, and we now have a prayer meeting over on campus.

Do you realize that everything got started because one girl was willing to pass out a funny book? Do you realize that you could give somebody one book, and it could cause thousands upon thousands of people to be saved? But unless you listen to the Holy Spirit, you aren't going to pass out tracts. As long as you listen to yourself, I will guarantee you that you will never pass out a tract. You never will.

But if you do listen, you will find yourself passing out tracts on planes, putting them in people's doors and laying them in public phone booths. Usually I will carry a few of them in my briefcase and just drop them everywhere. Sometimes when I get on a plane, I will put them in the magazine pockets on the backs of the seats in front of me, or sometimes I will just lay one on the seat next to me before somebody sits down in the seat, then they will have to pick it up.

I like that one little tract, *This Is Your Life*. Sometimes they will pick it up and flip through it then lay it back down, and I will ask them, "Can I see that?" And they will say, "Yeah, okay." So when they give it to me, I start reading it. When I get to about the third page, I say, "Humph, I wonder if this is really true?" Sometimes they will look at you funny, then I will read a couple more pages. Then I will say, "Boy, if this true, I had better get with it." Then I may turn to them and ask, "Do you believe this is true?" Sometimes they will clear their throat and say, "I don't know. What do you think?" And where it goes from there only God knows. I'm telling you the tract ministry can be something else.

What Will You Do?

How about you? Would you be willing to pass out a tract or knock on a door? Would you go to an open field and hold a meeting so a church could be built and a boy could be saved who would win others to Christ? You would be surprised how many Christians have never even won *one* soul to Christ!

What are you going to do, my brother or sister, when you stand before Almighty God, and He begins to hand out rewards according to your works? What are you going to do? Are you going to stand before Him empty-handed? I don't know about you, but I don't want to stand before God empty-handed.

The choice is yours. Jesus says, **Go out into the highways and hedges, and compel them to come in, that my house may be filled** (Luke 14:23). Are you willing to be led by the Spirit of God and obey Him? Are you willing to go anywhere for Him? Will you knock on at least one door and compel the people inside to come into the house of the Lord and listen to the Gospel being preached?

7

Never Stop Giving

Give, and it shall be given unto you.

Luke 6:38

If you were a businessman, how would the Spirit of God lead you? He would lead you according to what the Bible teaches you is for you. In God, there is no such thing as defeat, so He would lead you to be successful all the time. But if you don't put any emphasis on that and don't know how to be led by the Spirit of God in your business or in your life, then you won't always be successful.

Some people want to separate their business from their life, but it all works together you know. They say, "The Lord saved me and touched my life, so now I'm going to be a preacher. I just want to follow the Holy Ghost and give up everything."

You had better look at whether the Lord called you to preach and whether He is giving you that kind of a ministry.

"No, but I love Him, and I want to do what God wants me to do."

If the best thing in the world for you to do is what God wants you to do, then you need to find out what God wants you to do and do it. If He wants you to preach, then preach, but if He wants you to be a businessman, then be a businessman. Above all things, God wants you to be successful, not only spiritually but also financially. He wants you to be successful health-wise as well. The Spirit of God won't ever lead you any other way.

Any spirit leading you another way is not the Spirit of God because the Holy Spirit said He would lead you in line with His Word, and God wants you to live the abundant life. (John 10:10.) Jesus was led by the Spirit of God. When people obeyed the Bible and obeyed faith, then He responded. He does the same thing today. He responds.

Heed His Warnings

Now the Lord told me several years ago, "I want you to teach people what I've taught you. If you will, you will be more successful than you've ever been in every way."

One time in a service, Kenneth E. Hagin, a prophet of God, prophesied to me saying that the spirit of darkness, the devil, was going to attack my businesses. I didn't believe anything could happen to my businesses. But in the prophesy, he called my name and said that there wasn't anything wrong with any of my businesses. He said if I would pray and keep working for God and stay faithful to God and pray and pray and pray that I would come through that attack and would be more successful than I had ever been.

About six months after that, the devil hit my businesses. You talk about driving them broke! I am telling you, what the devil did was something else. He got into one of the secretaries who had been working for me for years, and she stole thousands and thousands and thousands of dollars from one of the corporations that I owned.

At midnight one night, the Spirit of God told me to go check the books, and I did. Then Holy Ghost showed me what she had been doing. After I caught her, I talked to the lawyer who said, "If you as a corporation press charges, the state will take the corporation over, and she will go to the penitentiary. You won't have anything to do with the company anymore because it will become a state corporation according to state law."

I didn't want to see the girl go to the penitentiary anyway, so I just backed away from it. I let her go then sold the corporation. The things that happened to me after Kenneth Hagin prophesied to me were amazing. If he had not prophesied to me, I don't know what would have happened.

Do you want to be successful? Then be led by the Spirit of God.

Be Led In Your Giving

Many people want to have money, whether they confess it or not. But most of them are not going to in any abundance. They will make enough money to pay their bills and buy food, but that will be about the extent of it because they simply aren't willing to be led by the Holy Spirit when it comes to their giving.

I was sitting in a prayer meeting one Wednesday night when the Spirit of God fell on me. There must not have been more than forty or fifty people there. The preacher preached, and a woman came to the altar and knelt down before God. Then the preacher said, "Everybody bow your heads now. We're going to pray." When we got through praying and I looked up, my eyes fell on this woman at the altar, and the Spirit of God came and overshadowed me. Then He spoke to me and said, "I want you to give that woman a hundred dollars and your table and chairs."

I didn't understand why He wanted me to do that at the time, but I understand now. So I grabbed my checkbook and wrote out a check for a hundred dollars. I was in a church awhile back when the Lord said that He wanted me to give someone a thousand dollars, so I gave it to them. Sometimes I have gone to places to speak, and the Lord has had me give them more than what they gave me.

I was crying so hard I couldn't even see the check. I was trying to wipe the tears away and write at the same time. I had just about written out the check when the Spirit of God spoke to me again and said, "Take it up there and give it to the pastor and tell him what I told you."

By the time I had written out the check, I was stumbling. I could hardly walk because I was getting blessed so much. So I stumbled towards the front and walked up behind the pulpit and said, "Pastor, Jesus told me to give this woman a hundred dollars and my table and chairs. Would you please have a truck come out to my house after the service and pick up my table and chairs?"

The devil will always tell you to put it off until tomorrow because he knows that if you put it off until then, you might get to thinking about it and say, "I don't want to do that. Why don't we talk this over?" So I said, "Bring a truck out to my house right away and load them up!" I didn't even know who she was.

That pastor knew me, and he said to the church, "I haven't talked to Brother Norvel today or for several days. He just came in the service, and he doesn't even know what he is doing." I said, "That's right."

Then he went on to say, "I found this woman today, and she has three little children, but she doesn't have even one slice of bread. She doesn't have any place for her children to sleep tonight. She's from Germany and is married to some flaky American soldier who ran off and left her. I just found them wandering around because she had to leave the place where she was living. Here she is in America with three little children, with no place to sleep. So I got her a motel room for the night so they could sleep, and I told them to come to church tonight."

If you want God to do something for you, go to church. If you aren't going to go to church, then you aren't going to get very much from God. I will tell you that right now. To receive anything from God, you have to make an effort to get to Him. Do you understand that?

So the pastor had brought her to church. He said, "If anybody wants to join Brother Norvel and give her some money, come up here and lay the money down." So they came up and started laying a whole pile of money down there for her. Then a woman rose up and said, "I have a chair I can give her." Then another person said, "I have a bed I can give her." Another person rose up and said, "I have two refrigerators; I can give her one of them." Another said, "I have a stove I don't need that I can give her."

Before the service was over, the girl said, "That fellow who came up here and gave me the hundred dollars — I want him to come up here and ask God to give me a job. Nobody wants to hire me because I have a heavy German accent and can't talk plain." So I went up there and laid hands on her and claimed a job for her. I said, "Satan, take your hands off of her employment, in Jesus' name. You thief!"

The devil has no right to your money! You have a right to it yourself. If you are a born-again Christian, you have a right for money to come in and pay all your bills. If you can hardly pay your bills, tell the devil to take his hands off of your money.

Ten days later, that pastor walked into my office and said, "I want you to take a ride with me." So we got in his car and drove by this little white house. Then the pastor said, "Do you remember about ten days ago when you were in my church and God moved on you to give a hundred dollars and your table and chairs to a woman?" I said, "Oh, yeah, I remember that." He said, "Well, she lives in that house right now, and all of her children are going to school. She has a job, and her refrigerator is full of food. Her house is full of furniture, and the blessing of heaven has fallen upon her." Now that sounds just like Jesus to me.

Bless Someone in Need

God loves an obedient child. **For as many as are led by the Spirit of God, they are the sons of God** (Rom. 8:14). That is the very reason why God did so much for the handmaidens of the Lord back in the Old Testament. We need to have handmaidens of the Lord now. What do you mean handmaidens of the Lord? I mean a woman who will just do anything for God. If a family is in trouble and is sick and doesn't have any food, she will go over and cook their meals, wash their sheets and love their children (and discipline them if needed) or do whatever needs to be done.

"I'm living in modern times, Brother Norvel. I don't have any friends who would do that, and I don't want to do that." Go ahead and be like your dumb friends then. You can be like them if you want to. But Jesus says that you can't give somebody a cup of cool water without Jesus rewarding you for it. (Matt. 10:41,42.) Water doesn't even cost anything, and you would get a reward. Just imagine what would happen to you if you would fix somebody a sandwich?

Love, the God-kind of love, reminds me of a boomerang — when you throw it out, it just comes back to you. That is the way the true love of God is. You throw it out, and it comes right back to you all the time. You aren't going to get very many blessings from heaven by living and breathing and taking care of your four and no more — you, your spouse, child and dog. But you will if you will give when you find people who are in need.

Go With God, Not the World

You have to watch yourself and not be led by the wrong spirit. You can't be led by a spirit of success. You can't be led by the spirit of making millions of dollars. You can't be led just by your talent. You can't be led by that kind of a spirit. The Holy Spirit of God wants to lead you, and you must learn to be led by the Holy Spirit of God.

Jesus always has souls, lost souls, in the back of His mind. He is always wanting you to obey the Gospel, but you have to pay the price to obey the Gospel. As far as the world is concerned, it isn't too popular to go preach the Gospel to every creature and cast out devils and speak with new tongues and lay hands on the sick so they will recover. But it is popular with Jesus, and He is the only One who matters anyway.

I couldn't care less what the world thinks. What they think isn't worth fifteen cents to me, and it shouldn't be to you either. But if you have anything to sell, they will try to buy you. They tried to buy me because I have a talent that the world would like to have, but I won't give it to them.

Now don't ask me why I have this talent because I don't know why. I am a high school dropout and don't even have a high school education, but by the age of twenty-eight years old, I was making about $5,000 a week. Ever since then, I have been successful and had money. There is just something inside of me that can see inside of a business, and I can make any kind of a business tick. I can take over the Cadillac dealership and make a success out of it. I can sell popcorn and make a success out of it. If I give some time to it, I know what to do, and I know how to do it.

Of course, the first key to being successful is to not be lazy, and I'm not lazy. God doesn't bless laziness. God doesn't bless lazy people. If you ever want to be successful in your life, you need to get out of that lazy seat because you aren't going to be successful as long as you are lazy. You can be baptized in the Holy Ghost and pray in the Spirit three hours a day, but if you are lazy, you aren't going to get the blessings from heaven. God wants to see people work. God likes to see you get up and get with it.

When I gave my life to God, I had one corporation making $3,000, $4,000, then $5,000 a week, but I was a slave to that corporation. My life didn't belong to God. My life belonged to my corporation. I had to work sometimes until eight, nine, ten, eleven o'clock at night. I had so much business I couldn't keep up with all of it. It just kept flowing in.

You would look at those checks and see $8,000, $10,000, $12,000, $15,000 a month. This week you would make $3,500 and next week you would make $5,500. This week you would make $4,000 and next week you would make $6,000. Now that wasn't bad for a Tennessee country boy who didn't have a high school education. Why, that is more than a governor makes!

You don't have to have a lot of education to make money, but you do have to be willing to work and do things, and God will bless you. He will bless your efforts just for working. God blesses people who work, but He doesn't bless laziness. He really doesn't. You have to pay a price to be successful.

When I gave my life to God, I had one business. Now I have seven, and I am never at work. That is what the Holy Ghost does to you. That is what He does for you. I can be riding down the road now sometimes, and the Spirit of God will come upon me and show me how to make $50,000 or $100,000. One time I even had Him come upon me and show me how to make a quarter of a million, and I made it too.

But after you make that, you still have to carry tracts in your pocket and know that it is important to pass out tracts, to lay your hands on sick people, to tell people about God, to cast out devils and to pray in the new language that God gives you. It is important to keep yourself built up spiritually so that you don't get full of pride and let your money control you.

My success and my business and my money don't control me. I control them. That is why I can teach the Bible for two months in a row nearly every day. That is the reason God dealt with me to start a Bible school. I teach certain subjects in the Bible school, and I have other teachers teaching in the Bible school. Can you imagine a guy who is a high school dropout starting a Bible school?

The Lord said, "Don't have any textbooks. Teach them the Bible by chapter and verse." So we don't have any textbooks, and we aren't going to have any unless God tells us to. The Lord told me to build a foundation in people in order to get the Word of God on the inside of their spirits so they could think straight. See, unless you get the Bible on the inside of you, your mind won't think straight. Your mind won't ever think straight until you make the Bible a part of you. It has to be in your spirit, and you have to see the value of winning a man's soul in order to stay successful.

Give Into Good Soil

You may be saying, "How did you get your Bible school to work? Why does God always send you everything you want? Why does your ministry account always have thousands of dollars, and you never have any problems? Why is that? Because I plant my seed in good soil. I give my money to ministries that are doing something for God. I believe in Kenneth Hagin's ministry, and I give into it and into his Bible school. And whenever I plant seed into his ministry, it multiplies like wildfire.

Realize that for seven years I worked in the ministry of helps. I used to carry food to poor people's homes. I would go buy the food myself then carry it to the homes of poor people who had little hungry kids who would tear the bottoms of the bags out before I could ever get the groceries out of the sack. Most of the time some flaky guy had left some woman with four or five little children, and they had no food.

I was satisfied with doing that because God was blessing me so much. I could hardly stand it! I mean, the joy of the Lord was surging through me day and night. Sometimes I would have to ask God to turn it off. One time I was in bed listening to a Bible reading tape, and God got to blessing me so much that I shook and the bed shook. God's joy surged through me so much that my bones started dancing. It almost seemed like there were little men dancing on my bones. Then your mind thinks, "I'm sure glad I'm in my bedroom alone." If the world had seen me, they would have thought I was nuts. They would have said, "He is having a fit." If they said that to me, I would say, "Yeah, I'm taking a fit. You ought to have one yourself. It feels good."

So the Lord blessed me, and He blessed my ministry. Then after working in the ministry of helps for seven years, the Lord said, "Now then, I want you to start teaching My Word." I didn't know God was ever going to call me to teach the Bible. I was satisfied in the ministry of helps. I was satisfied working to get money, then going out and spending it for God helping poor families. But He called me to teach the Bible.

Keep the Vision

Without a vision, God said, the people will perish. (Prov. 29:18.) You have to watch yourself and make sure you keep the vision God has given you. Now you might say, "Well, how does a man with seven businesses who doesn't need any money from anybody, how in the world does a man like that keep the vision of giving out the Gospel to win one soul for God? God showed me one time when I was in Tulsa, Oklahoma, getting ready to speak at a Full Gospel Businessmen's chapter meeting.

I was sitting on the side of a bed. I just held out my hands and began to pray, saying, "I love You, Jesus. I love You, Jesus. I just want to thank You, Jesus, for saving me." Then I said, "You know, Jesus, a few years ago, if I had been here in Tulsa, Oklahoma, on a Saturday afternoon I would have been buying the newspaper to see if anybody important was going to sing at some supper club so that I could go see them. Then I would have eaten a big steak and listened to somebody sing and watched a floor show.

But I said, "Jesus, why did I wait so long?" In just two or three hours, I'm going to go down to this fancy place, to speak to a room full of people, and I'm going to tell them what You've done for me. Why did I wait so long to give my life to You, Jesus? Why did I wait so long?"

Then all of a sudden, when I said that, He just came right through the wall and filled the whole room full of His Holy Presence. I got scared and backed up on the bed until my back was against the wall. The Spirit of God started fluttering and jumping in me, and I began to cry. Tears were just gushing out of my eyes. Then all of a sudden, I couldn't see.

Then my vision cleared, and I began to see the cross. God brought the cross that Jesus died on right up in front of my eyes. Jesus wasn't on the cross, but blood was dripping down the cross and onto me. He let me see the drops of blood with my eyes. And all the cross had on it was the stain from Jesus' blood.

Then He pushed it right up in front of me and said, "You didn't have a vision of the price that had been paid for your salvation and for your eternal life." He said, "People have lost the vision, son. The story of Jesus, the Easter story of Jesus dying on the cross, is like an old story they have read in some book somewhere, and they've lost the vision of the price that's been paid for them — death on the cross. They have lost the vision."

Did you ever sit down and stop and think that some Man died for you and nobody else. He died just for you. He went through that agony and suffered for hours in his body and in hell just for you. Then you and I have the audacity to stand up here and want to live our lives the way we want to. We fool around making money and looking at God and saying, "I don't want to get involved in this kind of stuff. I want to be a nice fellow. I'm going to find me a church that doesn't go so far."

You have to be out of your mind! You don't want to do that. You want the reality of God is what you want, but you just don't know it yet. When you get sick, my brother or sister, and cancer comes up on you, what are you going to do? What if Bright's disease attacks your kidneys like it did my nineteen-year-old brother's who played football in high school? What are you going to do? Are you going to go to your old, cold church? That is what we did, and he died at nineteen. Nobody could help him.

Today if I walked into the room of a nineteen-year-old football player in high school who was dying with Bright's disease or any other kind of disease, I would walk in there and say, "No, you don't! In Jesus' name; no, you don't! You foul affliction, you aren't going to kill this person. I'm not going to let you. In Jesus' name, I curse you, and I command every disease to come out of his kidneys in Jesus' name. Come out of him in Jesus' name."

You may say, "Why did you do that?" Because Jesus said in Mark 16:17, **In my name shall they cast out devils** and because the devil caused this Bright's disease to attack his kidneys, not God. So I had to take authority over the disease and command it to leave.

I don't know about you, but I would rather have a vision of the price that has been paid for me at times like these than to own the whole world.

Depend on God

Billy Graham says, and I agree with him, that the main problem with American people is that they haven't learned how to live yet. Billy Graham says that because American people are living in a land which flows with milk and honey and can go to the nearest supermarket and buy anything they want whenever they have some money in their pocket, they have become creatures of their own habits. If their values aren't in the right place and they don't know how to live and really be successful, then they become enslaved to their own habits. It becomes harder and harder for them to be led by the Holy Spirit and to find the reality of God because they are depending on themselves rather than on God. In Luke 6:38, God says, **Give, and it shall be given unto you; good measure, pressed down, and shaken together, and running over, shall men give into your bosom. For with the same measure that ye mete withal it shall be measured to you again.**

To really live, give yourself to God. Learn to depend on Him and be led by your spirit.

Norvel Hayes shares God's Word boldly and simply, with an enthusiasm that captures the heart of the hearer. He has learned through personal experience that God's Word can be effective in every area of life and that it will work for anyone who will believe it and apply it.

Norvel owns several businesses which function successfully despite the fact that he spends more than half his time away from the office, ministering the Gospel throughout the country. His obedience to God and his willingness to share his faith have taken him to a variety of places. He ministers in churches, seminars, conventions, colleges, prisons — anywhere the Spirit of God leads.

For a complete list of tapes and books
by Norvel Hayes, write:

Norvel Hayes
P. O. Box 1379
Cleveland, TN 37311

*Please include your prayer requests
and comments when you write:*

Other Books by Norvel Hayes

Divine Healing — God's Recipe For Life and Health

Worship

Confession Brings Possession

Let Not Your Heart Be Troubled

Endued With Power

How To Live and Not Die

The Winds of God Bring Revival

God's Power Through the Laying On of Hands

The Blessing of Obedience

Stand in the Gap for Your Children

How To Get Your Prayers Answered

Number One Way To Fight the Devil

Why You Should Speak in Tongues

What Causes Jesus To Work Miracles?

Visions — The Window to the Supernatural

Misguided Faith

What To Do for Healing

Financial Dominion — How To Take Charge of Your Finances

Rescuing Souls From Hell — Handbook for Effective Soulwinning

How To Cast Out Devils

Radical Christianity

Secrets To Keeping Your Faith Strong

Putting Your Angels To Work

Know Your Enemy

Available from your local bookstore.

Harrison House
Tulsa, OK 74153

For additional copies in Canada,
contact:

Word Alive
P. O. Box 670
Niverville, Manitoba
CANADA R0A 1E0

The Harrison House Vision

Proclaiming the truth and the power
Of the Gospel of Jesus Christ
With excellence;

Challenging Christians to
Live victoriously,
Grow spiritually,
Know God intimately.